MacArthur
IN THE PACIFIC

From the Philippines
to the Fall of Japan

Michael Green

Motorbooks International
Publishers & Wholesalers ®

This book is dedicated to my good friends Dennis Tomfohrde and Michael Haenggi
for all their help and support on this book.

First published in 1996 by Motorbooks International Publishers & Wholesalers, 729 Prospect Avenue, PO Box 1, Osceola, WI 54020-0001 USA

© Michael Green, 1996

Motorbooks International is a certified trademark, registered with the United States Patent Office

The information in this book is true and complete to the best of our knowledge. All recommendations are made without any guarantee on the part of the author or Publisher, who also disclaim any liability incurred in connection with the use of this data or specific details

We recognize that some words, model names and designations, for example, mentioned herein are the property of the trademark holder. We use them for identification purposes only. This is not an official publication

Motorbooks International books are also available at discounts in bulk quantity for industrial or sales-promotional use. For details write to Special Sales Manager at the Publisher's address

Library of Congress Cataloging-in-Publication Data
Green, Michael.
    MacArthur in the Pacific: from the Philippines to the fall of Japan/Michael Green.
        p. cm.
    Includes index.
    ISBN 0-7603-0202-2 (pbk.: alk. paper)
    1. MacArthur, Douglas, 1880-1964. 2. World War, 1939-1945—Campaigns—Pacific Area. 3. United States. Army—Biography. 4. Pacific Area—History, Military. 5. Generals—United States—Biography. I. Title.
D767.G74   1996
940.54'26—dc20   96-43575
ISBN 0-7603-0311-8

On the front cover: Five days after the formal Japanese surrender, MacArthur entered Tokyo and established his new headquarters in the center of the city. For the next several years MacArthur was virtual ruler of over 70 million people. He is pictured here leaving his Tokyo city headquarters. *MacArthur Memorial*

Back cover, top: This picture shows MacArthur aboard a borrowed jeep on the main landing beach at Luzon. Once the bulk of his ground forces were ashore, MacArthur's plan was to send a large portion of his forces down the central plain of Luzon to recapture his beloved city of Manila. He was convinced that the Japanese would not defend Manila and that he could retake all of Luzon within six weeks' time. Much like the capture of Leyte, which took far longer then he planned, the liberation of most of Luzon would take more than six months and cost almost 47,000 American dead and wounded. *MacArthur Memorial*

Back cover, bottom: Although the United States had maintained military forces in the Philippines since their annexation in 1898, the islands were largely unprepared for hostilities with Japan. This lack of preparedness was the result of several factors. As a signatory of the Washington Naval Treaty in 1922, the United States had agreed, in exchange for limitations on Japanese shipbuilding, to halt construction of any new fortifications in its Pacific possessions. For the Philippines this meant that only the islands near the entrance to Manila Bay, principally Corregidor, were well protected. Shown in this prewar picture are Philippine soldiers manning a 155-mm coast artillery gun during a training exercise. *U.S. Army*

Printed in the United States of America

CONTENTS

ACKNOWLEDGMENTS

Special thanks are due to the staff of the MacArthur Memorial located in Norfolk, Virginia, for their help and assistance on this book. Dr. Robert Wright and the staff of the U.S. Army Center for Military History in Washington, D.C., also provided assistance for this book. Other organizations that provided assistance were: the National Park Service, the Aberdeen Proving Ground Museum, the Patton Museum of Cavalry and Armor at Fort Knox, Kentucky, and the Armor School Library also located at Fort Knox, Kentucky.

Individuals who assisted with pictures and background material for this book include: Ron Hare, Glen Willford, Bob Cressman, George Shizmer, July Stephenson, Katie Tabot, Bill Nahmens, Roy Roberston, Roy Hamilton, Jeffrey MacKaughan, John Martini, Hideya Ando, Dean and Nancy Kleffman, Jim Mesko, Stephen Haller, Jacques Littlefield, Paul Handel, Milton Halsey, Kermit Bonner, Jr., Wally Peterson, and Richard Hunnicutt.

INTRODUCTION

One of America's best-known military leaders was General Douglas MacArthur. MacArthur's military career spanned three of America's major military conflicts of the 20th century: World War I, World War II, and the Korean War. Of MacArthur's long and varied career in the service of his country, this book will only cover the period between December 1941 through September 1945.

Due to space limitations and because this book is essentially a pictorial work, your author has condensed and summarized an important period of MacArthur's life into just under 50,000 words. These restrictions dictate that many aspects of a highly complex man who played an important role in this country's history are touched upon very lightly or skipped altogether. For those whose interest in MacArthur is sparked by this book and wish to learn more about the man and his life, there are a large number of published sources that delve into much more detail on his life.

History is interpreted many different ways by different people. The actions and decisions of important people in American history like MacArthur can be seen by some as heroic and selfless. Others may see the same actions as egotistical and self-serving. Any prejudices discerned by the reader in this book are those solely of your author, and are based on his research, and not those of the publisher.

Chapter One

THE JAPANESE ONSLAUGHT

On December 7, 1941, Japanese naval aircraft attacked Hawaii and left a great deal of the U.S. Navy Pacific Fleet at Pearl Harbor in flaming ruins. The Japanese decision to enter into a war with the United States was not a surprise to most people. Despite intense negotiations, relations between Japan and the United States had gone steadily downhill through mid-October 1941 and early November 1941 due to an American trade embargo of Japan. The trade embargo was America's way of punishing the Japanese for its conquest of so much of China.

Japanese Marines patrol the streets of a Chinese city in the 1930s. In late 1941, the military rulers of Japan were faced with the fact that their plans to conquer China (which had started in late 1931) had resulted in a war they couldn't seem to win or afford to lose. American political opposition to Japan's attempted conquest of China had grown to the point that President Roosevelt had slapped economic sanctions on Japan in January 1940. *Author's collection*

The level of Japanese discontent with the American trade embargo can be seen by the prewar statement of a high-ranking Japanese civilian official: "If the present condition is left unchecked . . . Japan will find itself totally exhausted and unable to rise in the future." This high-level civilian official, as well as most of Japan's military leaders, believed that the American trade embargo of Japan would bring about Japan's complete collapse within two years. The only response that many of Japan's political and military leaders saw to the American trade embargo was to go to war with the United States while their country still had the power to do so. In a 1949 interview, a member of the Japanese royal family stated, "Japan entered the war with a tragic determination and in desperate self-abandonment." His prewar belief was, "if Japan lost the war, there would be nothing to regret because she is doomed to collapse even without the war."

The Japanese themselves were never interested in conquering the United States. Their major reason for entering into a war with America was to assure Japan's conquest of southwest Asia. With the ownership of the natural resources present in that area of the world, Japan believed that it could establish a powerful defensive perimeter based in the Pacific that could deter America from ever attempting an attack on the Japanese Empire.

On November 24, 1941, the U.S. Navy issued a warning to both its own commanders in the Pacific as well as U.S. Army commanders that Japanese troop movements indicated "a surprise aggressive movement in any direction, including attack on Philippines or Guam" was a real possibility. On November 27, 1941, the U.S. Navy sent out an even stronger warning: "This dispatch," it read, "is to be considered a war warning . . . and an aggressive move by Japan is expected within the next few days." Navy commanders were alerted to the possibility that the Japanese Army with the support of the Japanese Navy might conduct amphibious landings operations against the Philippines. They were instructed to "execute an appropriate defensive deployments preparatory to carrying out the tasks assigned in their war plans."

For some reason, the top brass of the U.S. Navy never even considered the fact that the Japanese would try to attack Pearl Harbor. This belief is hard to understand when it is now known that the American Ambassador to Japan, Joseph C. Crew, had reported to Washington and the War Department as early as January 1941 that there "was talk in Tokyo of a surprise attack on Pearl Harbor." On November 3, 1941, Ambassador Crew warned Washington and the War Department that recent troop movements placed Japan in a position to begin military operations "in either Siberia or the Southwest Pacific or in both," and that war might come with "dramatic and dangerous suddenness."

The attack on Pearl Harbor on December 7, 1941, only confirmed what Ambassador Crew had feared. This attack plunged the United States not only into war with the Empire of Japan but also with Nazi Germany and Fascist Italy. America would be forced to fight a two-front war on a global scale.

The overall military outlook for the United States on December 8, 1941, was pretty grim for America's political and military leaders. Pearl Harbor had struck a crippling blow at the United States Navy in the Pacific. It had also caught the U.S. Army still engaged in carrying out a general mobilization plan.

The Threat to the Philippines

Immediately after Pearl Harbor, America's military leaders rushed what forces they had to the areas that seemed to be in the most danger of a Japanese invasion; these included the Panama Canal, Hawaii, the west coast of the United States, and the one area that was

Japanese Army troops in China prepare for an attack. Because of American economic sanctions, the Japanese were suffering serious shortages by June 1941. Japanese negotiations with other countries for the raw materials needed to keep its military forces in China going had failed. Having been backed into an economic corner of their own making, Japanese warlords decided in an act of desperation to use their military forces to seize the rich resources of east and southeast Asia. *U.S. Army*

in the most immediate peril, the Philippines. The man in charge of the Philippines defenses was America's best-known military hero from World War I, General Douglas MacArthur. What America's military leaders didn't know at the time was that the Japanese had no intentions of trying to invade Pearl Harbor or the western United States. Nor was the Panama Canal in any danger.

The only major American military outpost (other than Pearl Harbor) that stood in the way of the Japanese conquest of east and southwest Asia was the Philippine Islands, shown on this map. Of the 7,000 islands that make up the Philippines, the largest and most populous was Luzon. Luzon was also home to most of the American military forces based in the Philippines. The island was about 5,000 miles from Pearl Harbor and over 7,000 miles from San Francisco. The bad news for the American forces on Luzon in December 1941 was that Tokyo was less then 2,000 miles away. *U.S. Army*

Unlike Pearl Harbor or the coast of California, the conquest of the Philippines was a military necessity for Japan's military leaders. The Philippines was the only major American military outpost in that part of the world which could possibly slow down the Japanese Navy and Army from the capture of the immense natural resources (rubber, oil, and minerals) of the Dutch East Indies and Malaya.

The Japanese military leaders feared that given enough time, MacArthur could strengthen his forces sufficiently to make any possible Japanese invasion of the Philippines very difficult. In a postwar interview, a senior

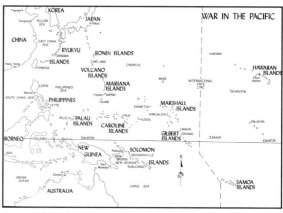

This map shows the South Pacific and the various islands and waters where action took place during World War II. When viewing the islands on a map like this one, it becomes clear how various island groups (i.e., the Carolines, the Philippines, the Marshalls, etc.) were regarded as strategic stepping stones by the respective parties involved in the war. The island groups were like positions on a chess board to the respective combatants, the Japanese and the Allied Forces.

Japanese officer stated, "If the Philippines were fortified and the defense strengthened by additional troops, Japan could not have undertaken war with the United States." A Japanese officer involved in the planning for the invasion of the Philippines in December 1941 stated in a postwar interrogation, "If there had been 50,000 additional men in the Philippines, and the defenses [had] been completed, we would have had to reconsider carefully the consequences of going to war."

MacArthur was no stranger to the Philippines. His father had been the famous General Arthur MacArthur who had bravely fought in the Civil War, the Indian Wars, and the Spanish American War. Landing in the Philippines with his troops soon after Commodore Dewey's victory over the Spanish fleet based in Manila Bay, Arthur MacArthur had led the decade-long battle against the Philippine freedom fighters who wished for independence from any foreign domination. In 1903, fresh out of West Point, newly commissioned Second Lieutenant Douglas MacArthur's first assignment was the Philippines.

The younger MacArthur's biggest claim to fame was due to his leadership skills and personal bravery under fire in France during World War I. MacArthur came home to the United States in 1919 as its second-most-decorated war hero.

MacArthur would return to the Philippines after his retirement from the U.S. Army on December 31, 1935. On his arrival in the Philippines in early 1940. MacArthur became the only field marshal in the Philippine Army. This rank did not exist in the American Army.

As the threat of war with Japan grew stronger in early 1941, MacArthur was returned to active duty in the U.S. Army on July 26, 1941, as commander of all military forces based in the Philippines.

World War II had actually started for much of the world in September 1939 with the German invasion of Poland. Most American military and civilian leaders had already seen the handwriting on the wall and knew it would only be a matter of time before they, too, would be dragged into the conflict. The U.S. War Department (now better known as the Department of the Army) had already activated 36 divisions and over 40 combat air groups even before the Japanese attack on Pearl Harbor. However, few were regarded as ready for combat in December 1941. The War Department had reported that it did not have more than two divisions trained and equipped to take part in any overseas operation. Even these forces could only be transported and supplied overseas when the U.S. Navy could regain control of the seas. In December 1941, it was hard for most Americans to believe that the United States would ever be able to produce the shipping, supplies, and military power necessary to push the Japanese out of the Pacific Ocean and at the same time help the other Allied nations throw back the Nazi war machine.

Even before the end of December 1941, American President Franklin Delano Roosevelt and British Prime Minister Winston Churchill, in conjunction with their top military leaders, had already decided that they would go on the offensive as soon as possible. Nazi Germany would be the number one enemy of the Allies with the Empire of Japan being a secondary target. MacArthur never accepted this choice and throughout World War II fought hard to convince both Washington and the American public that America's best interest was in defeating Japan first and not helping the British defeat Nazi Germany.

MacArthur and Roosevelt came from opposite sides of the political spectrum. What made

Given the task of defending the Philippines from a possible Japanese invasion was American military hero General Douglas MacArthur. Commissioned a second lieutenant out of West Point in 1903, MacArthur's military skills and family connections aided him in quickly rising through the ranks. By the time America entered World War I in April 1917, MacArthur was a major. By August 1917 he was promoted to full colonel and in June 1919 he attained the rank of brigadier general. In this picture we see Colonel MacArthur (far left) observing American troops in action near Glonville, France, in early July 1918. *MacArthur Memorial*

After World War I, family connections got MacArthur assigned as the superintendent of West Point. Because of a serious tiff between MacArthur and Army Chief of Staff General John J. Pershing in early 1922, MacArthur found himself transferred to the Philippines. In 1925, MacArthur was promoted to the rank of Major General (two stars) and returned to the United States. This picture taken in the 1920s shows MacArthur with two stars and his numerous decorations. During World War I, MacArthur won seven silver stars for his leadership abilities and bravery in battle. *MacArthur Memorial*

things even worse were MacArthur's complete lack of political subtlety, his incredibly large ego, and his very unhealthy belief in his own infallibility. The result was a deep political chasm between Roosevelt and MacArthur that led to an underlying tension between the two men throughout World War II.

MacArthur was convinced that he knew more then anybody else on how the American war effort should be conducted. MacArthur also firmly believed there was a conspiracy organized by President Roosevelt, the Joint Chiefs of Staff, and the State Department, and that they were deliberately doing all they could to prevent him from acquiring the means he needed to defeat the Japanese in the Pacific.

MacArthur and many powerful Republican midwestern politicians and businessmen in the United States so detested the political and military direction set by Roosevelt before and during World War II that there was an attempt in 1944 to place MacArthur's name on the list of possible presidential candidates for the Republican Party. MacArthur never technically said he would agree to such an effort. However, he never put a complete stop to it. Unfortunately, in the first primary election in which his named appeared on the ballot, his popularity with much of the American public didn't translate into votes. At that point, even his political supporters realized he had no hope of winning in any type of election.

The Japanese Attack

Once the Japanese military had decided to attack the Philippines, its first and most important target was MacArthur's land-based bombers. In early December 1941, MacArthur had under his command in the Philippines roughly 277 Army Air Corps planes. This was the largest concentration of American military planes outside of the United States. There were only 231 American military planes based at Pearl Harbor in early December 1941.

Of MacArthur's 277 planes, fewer then half were first-line combat aircraft. The best of the planes consisted of 35 early model B-17 bombers and about 54 P-40 Warhawk fighters. The Japanese considered the B-17 bombers the biggest threat to their plans since these aircraft had both the range and payload to attack Japanese military airfields on Formosa, or any invasion fleet approaching the Philippines.

American air strength in the Philippines had been closely watched by the Japanese, and it figured heavily in their military plans before Pearl Harbor. In a postwar interrogation of a Japanese officer involved in the attack on the Philippines, he stated: "We had estimated that there were 200 planes available to General MacArthur in the Philippines before the opening of hostilities. Had there been twice this

In 1929, MacArthur was appointed Chief of Staff of the United States Army by then-Republican President Herbert Hoover. Pictured is MacArthur (left) in full general's uniform in the summer of 1932. In March 1933 Democrat Franklin D. Roosevelt became president. By 1935, Roosevelt was looking to replace MacArthur with somebody more to his liking. Having held the Army's highest post, MacArthur felt that retiring from the service was his only option. *MacArthur Memorial*

Fortunately for MacArthur, as he faced the question of what to do with the rest of his life after retiring from the Army, his old Philippine family friend and business partner Manuel Quezon, soon to become president of the Philippines, asked him to return to the Philippines as the high commissioner. Since MacArthur wished to retain his ties with the U.S. Army, he went to the Philippines in 1935 as a military advisor. Pictured together are Quezon and MacArthur. *MacArthur Memorial*

On his return to the Philippines, MacArthur faced the daunting task of trying to build a Philippine military force strong enough to repel any potential invader. Pictured on his arrival in Manila in October 1935 is MacArthur in civilian clothes receiving military honors from an infantry unit. Standing behind MacArthur to the left, in civilian clothes, was Major Dwight D. Eisenhower, who spent some time on MacArthur's staff prior to the outbreak of the war. Eisenhower soon left MacArthur and the Phillipines to later become the Supreme Allied Commander in Europe during World War II. *MacArthur Memorial*

amount, I doubt that it would have been possible to attack the Philippines successfully. Had General MacArthur had this additional air power, the Japanese might not have been able to attack the Philippines at all, and possibly would have been unable to open hostilities elsewhere."

To prepare for their future assault on the Philippines in early December 1941, the Japanese military had amassed a force of almost 800 aircraft. On the morning of December 8, 1941, the Japanese launched 108 of their bombers escorted by 84 Zero fighter planes against the main American military airfield in the Philippines. Their target was Clark Field, located on the main Philippine island of Luzon. At 11:30 that morning, reports of the approaching Japanese formation began reaching Nelson Field, also in the Philippines. Further confirmation came from the two U.S. Army radar sets then operating in the Philippines. In addition to the radar reports, almost

Although the United States had maintained military forces in the Philippines since their annexation in 1898, the islands were largely unprepared for hostilities with Japan. This lack of preparedness was the result of several factors. As a signatory of the Washington Naval Treaty in 1922, the United States had agreed, in exchange for limitations on Japanese shipbuilding, to halt construction of any new fortifications in its Pacific possessions. For the Philippines this meant that only the islands near the entrance to Manila Bay, principally Corregidor, were well protected. Shown in this prewar picture are Philippine soldiers manning a 155-mm coast artillery gun during a training exercise. *U.S. Army*

Right
Besides the massive 12-inch barbette-mounted coast artillery guns found on Corregidor, there were also a large number of 6-inch, 10-inch, 12-inch, and 14-inch coast artillery guns mounted on disappearing carriages both on Corregidor and the other islands guarding Manila Bay. Pictured is a 12-inch disappearing gun. All these gun emplacements were built before World War I and were considered basically obsolete due to the lack of overhead cover both for the guns and their crews. When designed and built, these coast artillery guns did not face the threat from the air as they did in the 1940s. The idea for mounting large coast artillery guns on disappearing carriages came from a Scottish inventor in 1865. However, it was two U.S. Army officers who perfected the idea of using a gun's recoil, hydraulic buffers, and a counterweight to allow coast artillery guns to remain hidden behind cover until the moment they were fired. When fired, the gun's own recoil pushed it and its carriage to a level below that of any naval ship's observation. While under cover, the gun could be reloaded and prepared for its next target. This picture shows an example of a disappearing gun in the raised firing position. *U.S. Park Service*

The most impressive coastal defense fortification located in the entrance to Manila Bay was known as Fort Drum, shown in this prewar photo. Located 3 miles south of Corregidor, Fort Drum was built on a very small island known as El Fraile. After leveling the island, the U.S. Navy had built a blunt-nosed, square-sterned, battleship-shaped structure, 345 feet long, 135 feet wide, and 40 feet high. Its concrete walls were 36 feet thick. The roof of this huge concrete pillbox was 18 feet thick, making it strong enough to withstand any land, naval, or air bombardment. *MacArthur Memorial*

every Philippine postmaster located along the northwest coast of Luzon either phoned in or used his telegraph to alert the American Aircraft Warning Center on Luzon of the high-flying enemy bombers. It was clear at this point to the American officers at the aircraft warning center that the target for these enemy aircraft was Clark Field. Japanese planes had already struck targets in the Philippines that morning at about 9:30. Every American soldier, sailor, or Marine—from enlisted man to officer—stationed in the Philippines on the morning of December 8, 1941, knew from official warnings or civilian radio that the Japanese had struck Pearl Harbor the day before.

At roughly 11:45 that same morning, the American aircraft warning center sent a message by teletype to Clark Field to warn of an impending attack, followed by a telephone call. Some wartime sources contend that a radio warning also went out to Clark Field, but was never received because of jamming by the

Pictured during a prewar parade is MacArthur reviewing Philippine troops. American prewar military plans for defending the Philippines from a Japanese invasion (code named Plan ORANGE) had envisioned only a limited defense of Manila Bay and critical adjacent areas. If attacked, the U.S. Army garrison was expected to withdraw to the Bataan Peninsula, a tongue of land on Luzon forming the northwestern boundary of Manila Bay, and to the island of Corregidor. The U.S. Navy then sailed to the rescue as soon as possible. Nobody had foreseen the surprise attack on the Pacific Fleet at Pearl Harbor or the fact that the United States would be forced to fight a two-front war. *MacArthur Memorial*

Japanese. For whatever reasons (many of them unanswered to this day), when the Japanese bombers flew over Clark Field on December 8, 1941, almost all of MacArthur's fighters and bombers were neatly lined up in rows on the air field for easy destruction by the Japanese bombers and fighter planes. In postwar interviews, Japanese pilots who took part in that attack said they were "surprised to find the American aircraft lined up on the field."

In an attack that lasted about an hour, MacArthur lost the major portion of his air force. Eighteen of the B-17 bombers were destroyed as well as 53 P-40 fighter planes. Another 30 or so older-generation aircraft were also destroyed on the ground. Many of the planes that weren't totally destroyed were so heavily damaged that they were effectively put

Japanese troops are shown celebrating another conquest. The movement toward war accelerated on July 25, 1941, when Japan announced it had assumed a protectorate over French Indochina (now known as Vietnam). President Franklin D. Roosevelt immediately issued an executive order freezing all Japanese assets in the United States, denying to Japan its sources of credit, and cutting off imports of rubber, fuel, and iron. Roosevelt also responded by incorporating the Philippine forces into the U.S. Army and recalling then-retired General MacArthur to active duty as commander of U.S. Forces, Far East. *Author's collection*

Pictured on a prewar training exercise is a long column of American infantrymen in their World War I-style helmets and armed with bolt-action Springfields. Even before the Japanese assault on the Philippines began on December 8, 1941, the U.S. Joint Chiefs of Staff had already decided that in the event America went to war, it would adopt a defeat-Germany-first strategy. This meant that the American defenders of the Philippines would not be resupplied or reinforced once the Japanese began their assault on the Philippines. This fact was not known to American troops stationed in the Philippines in late 1941. *U.S. Park Service*

out of service for the rest of the campaign. Personnel losses were put at 80 killed and 150 wounded. The total Japanese loss for the day was only 7 fighter planes.

A military report done by the Provisional Tank Group assigned to guard Clark Field gives a vivid description of the Japanese attack on that day: "When word about Pearl Harbor came early morning 8 December, the crews were at the tanks, the tanks ready for action. At 0830, word came that 'hostile planes were forty minutes away.' All preparations were checked and the men stood by. At 1130 the planes which had taken to the air shortly after 0830, came in and landed, lining up conveniently to the mess. Tank headquarters learned subsequently that 'the alert had been called off.' The tankers were eating in the vicinity of their tanks at 1230, when a handsome V formation of fifty-three planes appeared from the north at between 20,000 and 23,000 feet; and almost as soon as discerned began bombing

Shown running at high speed in this prewar picture is the U.S. Navy battleship *California*. Many Americans believed powerful ships like this could deter any Japanese aggression in the Pacific. Unfortunately, Japanese military leaders felt that the loss of credit and essential natural resources needed to keep their economy going, and the threat of a substantial American military garrison in the Philippines left them with no choice other than to go to war against the United States. This was not an easy choice for many Japanese political and military leaders of the time. Many believed that a large-scale war with the United States was something they might not be able to win. *Real War Photos*

Clark Field. Only the 108 AA [antiaircraft] guns could be brought to bear, but their fire was of no effect at that range. The 108 37-mm and 432 .30-caliber guns of the tanks other than the AA guns were of no avail until the dive and glide bombing and strafing phase began. The open guns, .50 and .30 calibers, in half-tracks proved very useful although dangerous to serve. That day T/Sgt. Zemon Bardowski, B/192d, brought down the first enemy plane to the credit of the Armored Force in World War II. . . . The tanks, being hidden and camouflaged, were overlooked initially, in the enemy's concentration on the unconcealed [American] planes conveniently lined up."

Simultaneously with the attack on Clark Field, the Japanese also attacked Nelson Airfield on Luzon, and as at Clark Field, the American planes were caught on the ground and destroyed. The Japanese planes also managed to

U.S. Navy strength in the Philippines was reinforced in the six months prior to the Japanese invasion. On December 7, 1941, MacArthur could count on the 1 heavy and 2 light cruisers, 13 old destroyers, 32 long-range patrol planes, 6 gunboats, 6 PT Boats, and 29 submarines. Most of the submarines assigned to the Philippines were the obsolete S-type as shown here in this prewar picture at Pearl Harbor. *Real War Photos*

Pictured in a prewar training exercise are these American 155-mm long-range artillery guns and their towing tractors being loaded aboard flat cars. Although the number of American soldiers in the Philippines had been significantly reinforced by December 1, 1941, it still remained perilously inadequate for the task at hand. Its strength stood at only 31,095 men before the Japanese invasion of the Philippines began. *U.S. Army*

Pictured in a prewar training exercise is this mass formation of U.S. Army light tanks. Last-minute reinforcements sent from the United States to the Philippines consisted of the National Guard 200th Coast Artillery Regiment and the 192d and 194th Tank Battalions. These units arrived in the Philippines at the end of September 1941. Although these National Guard units had been hastily mobilized and were insufficiently trained in some areas, they brought with them some modern equipment, including 108 M3 light tanks, the first to reach the Philippines. *Patton Museum*

Shown in this official prewar U.S. Army photo is an M3 light tank fitted with all of its onboard weapons. The M3 light tanks shipped to the Philippines in late 1941 to bolster MacArthur's forces were the newest tanks in America's inventory at the time. Powered by a large aircraft-type radial air-cooled gasoline engine, the M3 light tank could reach a top speed of 36 mph. With a four-man crew, the tank was armed with a high-velocity 37-mm gun and as many as five .30-caliber machine guns. Armor protection averaged about a 1/4-inch-thick, and at thickest it measured about 1 1/2-inch on the front of the tank. *Patton Museum*

destroy a radar station and a number of military barracks and warehouses. On the following day, the Japanese attacked Nichols Field near Manila and destroyed many of MacArthur's planes that they had missed the day before. On December 10th, the Japanese planes attacked and destroyed the major American

naval yard on Luzon. Fortunately, most of the American naval vessels had left the Philippines on the evening of the 8th.

In only two days time, and to the utter amazement of the Japanese military leaders in Tokyo, Japanese bombers and fighter planes had almost completely destroyed MacArthur's air and naval power in the Philippines. Not only would MacArthur's forces in the Philippines have to fight without any air cover or support from the sea, but the Japanese conquest of other islands in the southern Pacific could go on without fear of American military interference.

The Japanese Landings Begin

Small units of the Japanese Army began landing on various islands of the Philippines as early as December 8, 1941. However, the main Japanese invasion force of 43,000 men wasn't landed until the morning of December 22 at Lingayen Gulf on the main island of Luzon. This location was about 100 miles from the Philippine capital city of Manila. Besides infantry, the Japanese landed artillery units and 100 tanks. Another smaller Japanese landing was made on December 23 at Lamom Bay, 200 road-miles southeast of the landing at Lingayen Bay. With the landing of this force, the Japanese plan was to attack Manila from both the north and south and trap MacArthur's forces in the middle.

To meet the Japanese invasion force, MacArthur had under his command a Philippine Army of 10 divisions plus support troops totaling approximately 100,000 men. Unfortunately, due to a lack of time, not a single Philippine Army division was up to full strength before the Japanese attack. None of these divisions had any antitank weapons and the shortage of artillery guns meant they were forced into battle without the firepower support they needed to face the Japanese invaders on even terms.

To aid in the training of his Philippine Army units, MacArthur had assigned at least 40 American officers and NCO's (non-commissioned officers) to each division. What value this might have provided the Philippine Army was mostly lost due to the language problem—not only between the American instructors and Filipinos but also among the Filipinos. This language problem can be seen in this wartime report: "The enlisted men of one division spoke the Bicolanian dialect, their Philippine officers spoke Tagalog, and the Americans spoke neither. In the Visayas, the problems were even more complicated since most of the officers were Tagalogs from central Luzon and the men spoke one or more of the many Visayan tongues. Transfers were made to alleviate the situation, but no real solution to the problem was ever found."

Even when the language problem could be overcome and training programs drawn up, there were almost no training facilities or equipment to train with in the Philippines. Many of the Philippine soldiers under MacArthur's command went into battle without ever having fired their weapons before.

Most of the weapons the Philippine Army had in its inventory tended to be either very old or just plain worn out. The standard rifle for the Philippine soldier was the American World War I–era .30-caliber Enfield rifle. There were also a number of old American 3-inch mortars in service. However, in combat, 70 percent of the mortar rounds were duds. One Philippine Army division managed to acquire eight World War I–era 75-mm guns on the evening of December 7, 1941. The only problem was that they came without sights or any fire-control equipment.

A more pressing problem with the Philippine Army under MacArthur's command was

Also sent to the Philippines along with the National Guard M3 light tanks were 50 M3 Gun Motor Carriages. These expedient tank destroyers were nothing more than a standard M3 armored personnel carrier (halftrack) mounting a World War I-vintage 75-mm field gun as shown in this prewar training photo. The gun itself was put on a pedestal mount in the center of the vehicle and provided with a thin armored shield to protect the gun crew. Armor protection on the halftrack was no more than a 1/4 inch at its thickest. The vehicle had a five-man crew and carried 56 75-mm rounds. *Patton Museum*

Pictured during a prewar training exercise in the Philippines is MacArthur (facing camera) conferring with Major General Jonathan M. Wainwright. By early December 1941 MacArthur had reorganized his growing command into four separate forces. The North Luzon Force, commanded by General Wainwright, defended the most likely sites for amphibious attacks and the central plains, the only suitable area for large-scale military operations. It also included the Bataan Peninsula, the designated fall-back position in the event of an American retreat. *MacArthur Memorial*

the poor quality of the officers. Even if the Philippine Army had been provided with all the equipment it needed, its officer corps was not up to the demands of combat. As the Japanese attack progressed, most of the Filipino officers were replaced with Americans.

The Philippine Army was backed up by a small American military contingent of about 25,000 soldiers. Most of these soldiers were based on the main island of Luzon. Of the 25,000 American soldiers, about 7,329 were assigned to infantry units. Another 4,967 men were assigned to the coast artillery guns that protected Manila Bay and Subic Bay from a possible Japanese naval attack.

MacArthur's largest infantry unit on Luzon was the Philippine Division, commanded by Major General Jonathan M. Wainwright. Except for one unit and a few military police and headquarters troops, all the enlisted men of the division were Philippine Scouts. In contrast to the Philippine Army, the Philippine Scouts was an elite unit of mostly career soldiers that had a very high esprit de corps. Intensely loyal to the United States and its units, they were also better educated than the typical Philippine or American soldier, well-trained, and somewhat better equipped than the regular Philippine Army divisions. The Scouts tended to think of themselves as more American than Filipino. The Scouts would prove to be MacArthur's best troops during the fight for the Philippines.

Despite the many shortcomings of the forces under his command, MacArthur had convinced himself that the Philippines could be defended from Japanese offensive action. His prewar belief in this matter can be seen in a 1936 speech in which he stated, "no Chancellery in the World, if it accepts the opinions of the military and naval staffs, will ever willingly make an attempt to willfully attack the Philippines." The islands, MacArthur pointed out, had "enormous defensive advantages in their geographical separation from possible enemies, mountainous character, heavy forests and jungles, narrow beaches and limited communications."

Luzon, the probable objective of an enemy, he reminded his listeners, had only two areas in which "a hostile army of any size could land.

Pictured on the move is a formation of Japanese Type 97 Tankettes. Armed with a 37-mm gun, the vehicle had a two-man crew. Japan's ambitious strategic plan in the Pacific and the continuing war in China sharply limited the size of the force available for the invasion of the Philippines. The Japanese high command assigned General Masaharu Homma, Commander of the 14th Army, the task of conquering the Philippines. Under his command were two infantry divisions, two tank regiments, an air group, plus the normal number of service and supporting troops. *Author's collection*

Each of these is broken by strong defensive positions, which if properly manned and prepared would present to any attacking force a practically impossible problem of penetration."

When the development of the Philippine Army was completed by 1946, MacArthur believed it would be strong enough to oppose successfully "any conceivable expeditionary force. It would have a great advantage also in being assigned only one mission: defense of the homeland. Each unit of the army would operate over ground it knew well and which had been deliberately selected and organized for defense."

MacArthur explained the absence of a Philippine Navy in his plan of defense thusly: "The major duty of a large navy was to protect overseas possessions. For the Philippines, which had no colonies, the only naval task was that of inshore defense. This defense would be provided by flotillas of fast torpedo boats, supported by an air force whose task would be to deny the enemy an opportunity to bring its forces close enough to Philippine shores to debark his troops and supplies."

Reality Sets In

MacArthur's prewar speeches came back to haunt him as soon as Japanese troops landed in the Philippines. He was quickly told by one of his field commanders that his men didn't stand a chance against the attacking Japanese forces and the field commander requested permission to withdraw. A message by

On the morning of December 7, 1941, over 360 Japanese planes attacked Pearl Harbor, home of the United States Navy's Pacific Fleet. Within a two-hour period the Japanese naval aircraft sank 3 battleships, capsized 1, and damaged 4 more. This picture shows the damage done to some of the Navy's battleships. In addition to the battleships, 3 light cruisers, 3 destroyers, and miscellaneous other vessels were badly damaged. The U.S. Army lost a total of 96 planes, ranging from fighters to bombers. *Real War Photos*

Japanese Marines are pictured leaving their assault boat. The first Japanese landing in the Philippines took place on December 8, 1941, the same day their planes had destroyed most of MacArthur's air force on the ground. Japanese landings continued to occur at various places throughout the Philippines until December 22, 1941, when the main Japanese landing took place on Luzon, about 100 miles away from the Philippine capital city of Manila. *Author's collection*

MacArthur to that same officer describes his feelings at that moment: "There is no position that we can take that will shorten your line except the mere beach-head. Were we to withdraw to such a line now it would not only invite immediate overwhelming enemy attack but would completely collapse the morale of our own force. Sooner or later we must fight to the finish. Heretofore we have been maneuvering, falling back from position to position until we have now reached our last ditch. Our only safety is to fight the enemy off."

At the same time he was asking his commanders to hold off the Japanese invasion forces, MacArthur sent a message to Washington informing the military leaders of his problems and concerns: "In Luzon, the enemy has landed fresh troops in the Subic Bay area and is attacking in force along my left and along the coast at many points. His coastal thrusts are covered by Navy warships and air force. I am counterattacking these landings on my

right to relieve the pressure by diversion but the worn condition of my troops pitted against the fresh units of the enemy makes the result hazardous. There is little that I can do except to try to stabilize the situation by the ferocity of my fighting. I am doing everything possible along this line."

Soon after this message was sent, even MacArthur began to realize his troops stood no chance against the Japanese forces arrayed against them. In another message to Washington, MacArthur described his plans to slow down the Japanese invasion force: "Heavy fighting has been raging all day. The enemy has been repulsed everywhere. He seems to have finally adopted a policy of attrition as his unopposed command of the sea enables him to replace at will. My losses during the campaign have been very heavy and are mounting. They now approximate thirty-five percent of my entire force and some divisions have registered as high as sixty percent. My diminishing

From their landing ship, Japanese soldiers observe a burning Philippine town. Having complete air and naval supremacy the Japanese forces in the Philippines made swift progress against MacArthur's forces. By December 23, 1941, MacArthur had already decided to fall back to Bataan and fight a delaying action there until help could arrive. By January 7, 1942, the bulk of MacArthur's force (80,000 men) had set up defensive positions on the Bataan Peninsula. *Author's collection*

strength will soon force me to a shortened line on which I shall make my final stand. I have personally selected and prepared this position and it is strong. With its occupation, all maneuvering possibilities will cease. I intend to fight it to complete destruction. This will still leave Corregidor."

The Retreat Begins

MacArthur had decided to withdraw most of his forces into the mountainous peninsula of Bataan. This called for a complex retrograde movement. Under constant enemy attack, MacArthur and his commanders completed the withdrawal by January 7, 1942. MacArthur sent a message to Washington describing his actions: "In Luzon: Under the cover of darkness I broke contact with the enemy and without the loss of a man or an ounce of materiel, am now firmly established on my main battle position. The execution of the

Pictured shortly after the Japanese landings in the Philippines, a grim-faced MacArthur, accompanied by some of his senior officers, visited some of Bataan's defensive positions. Only 25 miles long and 20 miles wide at its base, the Bataan Peninsula juts out from the mainland of Luzon. Mountainous and covered by thick jungles, the Bataan Peninsula had only two roads suitable for wheeled or tracked vehicles. While it offered MacArthur's troops some excellent defensive positions to hold off the invading Japanese forces, there was no room for maneuver and no place to retreat. *MacArthur Memorial*

As the Japanese military forces approached the city of Manila near the end of December 1941, MacArthur decided to move his family and staff to the relative safety of Corregidor. Many high-ranking members of the Philippine government followed MacArthur to the island. Pictured sitting together on Corregidor are MacArthur and Philippine President Manuel Quezon. For reasons known only to himself, MacArthur only left Corregidor one time to visit his men on Bataan. This decision did much to destroy the morale of the trapped American and Philippine soldiers on Bataan. *MacArthur Memorial*

Japanese troops rush into the attack. American soldiers fighting in the Philippines learned that Japanese soldiers normally preferred to attack defensive positions under cover of darkness. Japanese offensive operations normally began with a feint at one place to draw attention while the real attack would begin in another location. Instead of using runners or radios, Japanese soldiers would sometimes keep alignment at night by using a drummer who regulated the advance by different beats of a drum. *Author's collection*

movement would have done credit to the best troops in the world."

MacArthur's message to Washington stating that he hadn't lost a man or any supplies during his forces' withdraw to Bataan wasn't completely accurate. During the withdraw to Bataan, close to 12,000 of his Philippine Army soldiers deserted their units rather then continue a fight they saw no chance of winning. Even worse was the fact that not enough food had been sent to Bataan before the withdraw began. Almost 10 million pounds of rice located in Philippine government warehouses that was supposed to be sent to Bataan to feed MacArthur's troops was lost because permission to move it to Bataan was not received in time. Even harder to believe is that MacArthur's staff forbid, under penalty of court-martial, the seizing of any food or clothing that belonged to Japanese-owned firms in the Philippines.

Pictured are Japanese soldiers carrying their wounded in field-expedient stretchers. The typical Japanese soldier was about 5-feet 3-inches tall and weighed around 116 pounds. He was paid $1.26 a month, of which he was allowed to spend nine and a half cents on himself. Japanese soldiers could live on a handful of rice and a few scraps of dried fish a day. It was not uncommon for Japanese soldiers to march 30 miles, with full pack, in a 24-hour period. American soldiers, who saw combat in the Pacific considered the Japanese soldier one of the toughest fighting men in the world. *Author's collection*

By January 2, 1942, the Japanese occupied Manila, the capital of the Philippines, which had been declared an open city on December 24, 1941. MacArthur's Luzon force was practically intact, but it was trapped in Bataan and on Corregidor and three small neighboring islands in Manila Bay. MacArthur had already moved his staff and family on to Corregidor on December 24, 1941. MacArthur's move to the relative safety of Corregidor caused many of his troops to begin referring to him as "Dugout Doug."

Manila Bay, one of the finest natural harbors in that part of the world, opens out from a 12-mile-wide entrance between high headlands. The bay expands toward the low-lying plain to a width of 30 miles. On either side of the entrance to Manila Bay are high volcanic peaks then covered with luxuriant tropical foliage. North of the entrance is the Bataan

Philippine Scouts, MacArthur's best soldiers, proudly display a captured Japanese officer's sword taken in battle. The Japanese began their assault on MacArthur's (approximately) 80,000 troops trapped on Bataan on January 9, 1942. It started with a massive artillery barrage which, according to a U.S. Army report, "shook the northern portion of the Bataan Peninsula." As soon as the artillery barrage lifted, Japanese infantry began moving forward. Despite Japanese beliefs that their attacks would be met by only light opposition, the Japanese main assault force was thrown back in a series of very bloody battles. *MacArthur Memorial*

peninsula; to the south is Cavite Province. From a military point of view, the more important and most easily defended was the headlands of the Bataan peninsula, a rocky extension of the Zambales mountain range, which separates the central plain of Luzon from the China Sea.

Across the entrance to Manila Bay are a number of small islands. The largest and most

Despite the U.S. troops' withdrawing to their backup defensive positions on Bataan on January 24, 1942, the Japanese attacks continued without pause for another two weeks. Mounting casualties finally convinced the Japanese commander in the Philippines that he couldn't break through the defending American and Philippine soldiers on Bataan with his existing military strength. A call went out for reinforcements, which poured into the Philippines throughout late February and early March 1942. By mid-March 1942, the Japanese were ready for their final assault on the defenders of Bataan. Pictured are Japanese tankers taking a break from the heavy fighting on Bataan. *Author's collection*

Japanese infantry attack an American-built M3 light tank. Notice the Japanese officer with his sword in the foreground. The sword was often carried by Japanese officers in the field as both a symbol of authority and as a weapon. It wasn't until January 15, 1942, that the Japanese main force managed to break through MacArthur's front line positions on Bataan. MacArthur therefore ordered his troops on Bataan to withdraw to their backup positions on January 24, 1942. *MacArthur Memorial*

important was the heavily fortified and armed island of Corregidor, which lies two miles off Bataan. Right next to Corregidor was the smaller, less-fortified island of Caballo which separated the entrance into Manila Bay into the North and South Channels. South of the islands of Corregidor and Caballo, and closer to Cavite Province, was the heavily fortified island of El Fraile, located in the opening of Manila Bay. These small islands located at the entrance to Manila Bay gave them a strategic importance out of all proportion to their size. In the history of American plans for the defense of the Philippines, these islands loomed very large.

From Bad to Worse

General MacArthur sent a message to Washington in January 1942, describing his assessment and frustrations with the numerous problems facing his command in trying to hold back the Japanese offensive operations in the Philippines: "The food situation here is becoming serious. For some time I have been on half rations and the result will soon become evident in the exhausted condition of the men. The limited geographical area which I occupy offers no food resources. I am entirely dependent upon a line of sea communications, the responsibility for which has not been under my control. In my radio message of January four I asked for blockade running ships. No reply has been received. . . . Unquestionably ships can get through but no attempt yet seems to have been made along this line. This seems incredible to me and I am having increasing difficulty in appeasing Philippine thought along this line. They cannot understand the apparent lack of effort to bring something in. I cannot overemphasize the psychological reaction that will take place unless something tangible is done in this direction. . . . I am professionally certain that his so-called blockade can easily be pierced. The only thing that can make it really effective is our own passive acceptance of it as a fact. I repeat that if something is not done to meet the general situation which is developing the disastrous results will be monumental."

Philippine President Manuel Quezon, a long-time friend and business associate of

By the middle of March 1942, the Japanese had begun moving large numbers of fresh troops into their positions on Bataan. Japanese aircraft began aggressively attacking anything that moved on Bataan. Among the armored vehicles employed by the Japanese Army in the Philippines was the Type 89B medium tank such as the one shown here on display at a U.S. Army museum. Developed in the early 1930s, the 15-ton medium tank first saw service in China in 1934. With a crew of four men, the vehicle had a top speed of 17 mph and was powered by a six-cylinder inline diesel engine. The tank was armed with a single 57-mm gun and two 6.5-mm machine guns. *Michael Green*

MacArthur, was so upset with the lack of military aid from the United States that he wrote in a February 8, 1942, letter to President Roosevelt: "The situation of my country has become so desperate that I feel that positive action is demanded. Militarily it is evident that no help will reach us from the United States in time either to rescue the beleaguered garrison now fighting so gallantly or to prevent the complete overrunning of the entire Philippine Archipelago. My people entered the war with the confidence that the United States would bring such assistance to us as would make it possible to sustain the conflict with some chance of success. All our soldiers in the field were animated by the belief that help would be forthcoming. This help has not and evidently will not be realized. Our people have suffered death, misery, devastation. After two months of war not the slightest assistance has

The newest Japanese tank to see action during the Japanese invasion of the Philippines was the 13-ton Type 97 medium tank. Built by Mitsubishi, the Type 97 was first deployed in Japanese service in 1937. Considered one of the best Japanese tank designs in the early years of World War II, the Type 97 was armed with a turret-mounted 57-mm gun and two 7.7-mm machine guns. With a four-man crew and powered by a diesel engine, the Type 97 had a top speed of 25 mph and an operational range of 130 miles. *Patton Musuem*

been forthcoming from the United States. Aid and succor have been dispatched to other warring nations such as England, Ireland, Australia, the N.E.I. and perhaps others, but not only has nothing come here, but apparently no effort has been made to bring anything here. The American Fleet and the British Fleet, the two most powerful navies in the world, have apparently adopted an attitude which precludes any effort to reach these islands with assistance.

"As a result, while enjoying security itself, the United States has in effect condemned the sixteen millions of Filipinos to practical destruction in order to effect a certain delay. You have promised redemption, but what we need is immediate assistance and protection. We are concerned with what is to transpire during the

Japanese artillery guns concentrated on trying to knock out American and Philippine front-line defensive positions. Another important target for both Japanese artillery and aircraft was the destruction of MacArthur's larger artillery pieces like the 155-mm M1918 howitzer, such as the one shown here in this prewar photo. Based on the design of a World War I-era French weapon, the M1918 howitzer was employed in the Philippines as both a coast artillery weapon as well as a heavy counter-battery weapon. As a mobile gun, the M1918 was towed by either a large truck or a fully-tracked artillery tractor. The gun could throw a 95-pound high-explosive round to a maximum range of 17,400 yards. *U.S. Army*

Somewhere on Bataan, the Philippine crew of this U.S. halftrack mounting a 75-mm antitank gun waited for the next Japanese attack. On April 3, 1942, the Japanese launched their final assault on Bataan with a massive five-hour artillery barrage supported by aircraft. American and Philippine defensive positions were churned into a worthless and useless mess. As soon as the supported fire ended, the Japanese sent in both their tanks and infantry to break through anything left standing. While some of the defending Philippine units tried to withdraw in an orderly fashion, many other units fled their positions in disorganized and unruly mobs. *Author's collection*

By April 8th, the Japanese had almost complete control over Bataan. On April 9, 1942, the American commander of Bataan surrendered his 78,000 men to the local Japanese commander. While MacArthur had ordered that surrendering to the Japanese was prohibited under any conditions, the U.S. Army commanders on the scene knew that their starving, exhausted, and disease-troubled troops were totally incapable of the physical effort necessary to even defend themselves, let alone counter-attack the Japanese forces arrayed against them. This wartime Japanese picture shows surrendered American and Philippine troops on Bataan. *MacArthur Memorial*

Shown on Corregidor is MacArthur (with cane) and his chief of staff Colonel Richard K. Sutherland coming out of the island's main underground tunnel for a walk. The forces on Corregidor Island had weathered the blockade better than those on Bataan. They had proportionately more supplies, and an extensive tunnel system affording protection from Japanese artillery and aerial bombardment. Nevertheless, by mid-April 1942, the defenders of Corregidor were also showing the effects of a prolonged siege. Although fortifications and gun emplacements had withstood the bombardment fairly well, the island's installations in the open, such as barracks, warehouses, water tanks, and the power plants, were highly vulnerable to Japanese air and artillery bombardments. *MacArthur Memorial*

The largest antiaircraft gun in service with MacArthur's troops on Luzon, Bataan, and Corregidor Island was the 3-inch gun such as the one shown here in a prewar training exercise. Based on an obsolete World War I naval design, the Army's 3-inch gun could fire a 12.7-pound high-explosive shell 14,200 feet straight up. Sadly for MacArthur's antiaircraft gunners, the ammunition provided for the 3-inch guns was so old that most of the rounds fired at Japanese planes turned out to be duds. *U.S. Park Service*

After the fall of Bataan, the combined Japanese aerial and artillery bombardment of Corregidor managed to knock out all the major American coast artillery guns and mortars. The only effective long-range artillery weapon left to the troops on Corregidor consisted of roughly 32 World War I-era mobile 155-mm guns. After being placed in a concealed position, these guns fired about 20 rounds of counter-battery fire and then moved out before the Japanese could pinpoint their location. Pictured in a Corregidor tunnel is a dejected-looking MacArthur, no doubt pondering what the future held for him and his family. *MacArthur Memorial*

next few months and years as well as with our ultimate destiny. There is not the slightest doubt in our minds that victory will rest with the United States, but the question before us now is: Shall we further sacrifice our country and our people in a hopeless fight? I voice the unanimous opinion of my War Cabinet and I am sure the unanimous opinion of all Filipinos that under the circumstances we should take steps to preserve the Philippines and the Filipinos from further destruction."

Extracts from a wartime report describe what was happening on Corregidor: "Bombing was resumed on December 31 and continued through January 7, 1942. . . . The enemy apparently was area bombing as bomb craters were uniformly scattered over the entire island. A crater could be found within a radius of twenty-five yards on any part of the island. Ammunition expenditure reports and planes brought down showed that it took about 120 rounds to bring down one plane. . . . With the bombers flying at 20,000 to 30,000 feet, it was found that gun batteries were able to get in about ten salvos before the planes were out of fuze range. . . . The bombing was followed by considerable looting on the part of Filipino and American soldiers. . . . In February the enemy made a landing on the west coast of Bataan in the rear of the main line of resistance. Battery Geary, 12 inch mortars, took under fire these enemy troops. . . . The 670 pound personnel shells with instantaneous fuze proved very effective. The prisoners thought the shells were bombs."

As things got worse on Bataan and Corregidor, MacArthur sent another message to Washington: "My estimate of the military situation here is as follows: The troops have sustained practically 50 percent casualties from their original strength. Divisions are reduced to the size of regiments, regiments to battalions, battalions to companies. Some units have entirely disappeared. The men have been in constant action and are badly battle worn. They are desperately in need of rest and refitting. Their spirit is good but they are capable now of nothing but fighting in place on a fixed position. All our supplies are scant and the command has been on half rations for the past month.

"It is possible for the time being that the present enemy force might temporarily be held, but any addition to his present strength will insure the destruction of our entire force. We have pulled through a number of menacing situations but there is no denying the fact that we are near done. Corregidor itself is extremely vulnerable. . . . Since I have no air or sea protection, you must be prepared at any time to figure on the complete destruction of this command."

No Glory Left

For the starving American soldiers trapped on Bataan who saw little or no glory in fighting a hopeless delaying action against the Japanese, a very catchy little tune was sung that did much to explain their feelings at the time: "We're the battling bastards of Bataan; No mama, no papa, no Uncle Sam; No aunts, no uncles, no cousins, no nieces; no pills, no planes, no artillery pieces. . . . And nobody gives a damn."

As MacArthur's troops began to lose heart over the situation in which they found themselves, MacArthur's messages to his commanders became shriller in tone: "All officers and men must be impressed with the fact that this is our last stand. *HERE IS WHERE WE WIN THE WAR.* Get rid of the cowardly fool idea that a small group of infiltrating Japs can 'cut off' any important element of this command. Reverse the viewpoint and consider any infiltrating group as easy victims to be immediately

surrounded and captured or destroyed. The 11th Division front has never been cracked yet. *We are going to hold on this line.*"

A description of what life was like for some of the American soldiers trapped on Bataan comes from the operational reports of the Provisional Tank Group: "Orders were given for the tanks to move under their covering detachment, as above, at dark, to a bivouac area south of Abucay-Abucay Hacienda road. Both tanks and men were in desperate need of rehabilitation. Tracks had been worn down to the metal. The great radial aviation-type motors were long past their essential 400 hours overhaul. In the course of the month's operation it had been necessary on the constant movement, or anticipated movement, to keep motors running or idling for protracted periods. Batteries were in parlous state. If the tanks were to survive they had to have maintenance. The same applied to the officers and men. And with half-rations, of a sort-mostly Filipino, beginning 6 January the men were already feeling the loss of food. Eyesight was notably impaired. . . . While the 192d (less a company) was working on the West Coast, attached to the I Corps, its companies had to be rotated with the reserve company (at Group Headquarters), successively rehabilitated and overhauled. By March the Surgeon reported the daily ration amounted to but 950 calories. Each battalion had so many sick with dengue and malaria that emergency battalion dispensaries took care of the men that were too badly off to get to the base hospitals. Three types of worms contributed their share of misery. . . . Gas allowance for all purposes other than tanks was cut to fifteen, then to ten gallons a day per battalion, making the prosecution of reconnaissance, contact, administration, and services about impossible. The armored troops had been ordered by Group on 27 January, to support in every way the defense, forgetting conventional tank employment; using tanks as pill-boxes in the front line, if required. The half-tracks were so big as to defeat their purpose in close country and on narrow, congested trails. They offered little protection and invited fire."

Despite the hardships endured by the American tankers of the Provisional Tank Group they still managed to take a heavy toll on the attacking Japanese forces. The following extract from a wartime report describes a single action of the Provisional Tank Group on Bataan: "The tanks in the 194th sector were still in a covering position about a kilometer north of the Pilar-Bagac road at about 0945 when a Filipino civilian came through the lines with the information that a considerable body of the enemy, in several columns, was approaching. Our troops were all behind the Bani road by 0400; but two of our tanks were lost through a bridge and by bombing and had not yet been salvaged. Major Ganahl's four SPM's [halftracks armed with a 75-mm gun apiece] were with the 194th, stationed on the flanks. When the enemy columns appeared

Knowing that the Philippines was doomed and that no military relief could be sent, President Roosevelt and his advisors felt it was unwise to leave MacArthur on Corregidor to be captured by the Japanese. On February 22, 1942, President Roosevelt gave MacArthur a direct order to evacuate Corregidor. Originally, it was planned that MacArthur, family, and staff left Corregidor by submarine. Eventually, it was decided by MacArthur to leave by PT-Boat. MacArthur, his family, and staff left Corregidor on March 11, 1942. After a harrowing 560-mile trip through Japanese-patrolled waters, MacArthur was transferred to a B-17 bomber and flown to Australia. Pictured is the type of PT Boat that took MacArthur off Corregidor. *Real War Photos*

The Japanese began their final assault on the island of Corregidor with a heavy artillery barrage on May 1, 1942. By May 5, the Japanese artillery in conjunction with its air force units had destroyed most of Corregidor's remaining mobile guns and searchlights. On the night of May 6, 1942, the Japanese sent in their infantry on landing boats. Shown in this wartime Japanese picture is their standard powered-landing barge as used in the Philippines throughout World War II. *Author's collection*

through the brush, every weapon, unit and personnel was brought to bear on the columns in close formation. Of an estimated 1,200, at least 500 were casualties. The fight and following fire, as the enemy abandoned its mission and fled, lasted forty-five minutes. Had this force hit the scarcely occupied, let alone organized, main position at this time, there is little likelihood that they could have been stopped. Their air retaliation came promptly, hitting the tanks' withdrawal as it was on the Orion Cut-Off south of the Pilar-Bagac road. Their bombing was wild and their strafing gingerly executed both with small effect."

On the night of March 11, 1942, Mac-Arthur left the island of Corregidor for Australia under orders from President Roosevelt. For most of the American soldiers, sailors, and Marines left in the Philippines to fight a hopeless delaying action, the departure of their commander-in-chief from the battlefield left a lot of bitterness that can still be found today among the aging veterans of that campaign who managed to survive Japanese POW (prisoner-of-war) camps.

Unlike those Americans left behind in the Philippines to be killed or captured by the Japanese, the American public, hungry for a hero, decided that MacArthur's escape from Corregidor to Australia was a great victory over the Japanese. This belief was no doubt aided by MacArthur's inaccurate but always dramatic press releases. MacArthur's powerful friends in the American newspaper publishing business also helped to spread the belief that MacArthur was a military genius. If the American public had been fortunate enough to have had alternative sources of information about MacArthur's activities in the Philippines, MacArthur's career might have taken a much different path.

MacArthur arrived in Australia on March 17, 1942. From his own wartime reports comes this graphic account of the event: "Departed from Corregidor at dark on the 12th making the trip with four U.S. Navy motor torpedo boats. Air reconnaissance revealed one hostile cruiser and one destroyer off the west coast of Mindoro but we slipped by them in the darkness. The following day was passed in the shelter of an uninhabited island but we risked discovery by air and started several

On the night of May 6, 1942, another wave of Japanese landing boats approached Corregidor. This time the heavy 12-inch mortars of Corregidor and the other islands defending Manila Bay opened fire, as did the remaining 3-inch and 75-mm guns. Japanese observers on the scene described it as if "a hundred guns rained red-hot steel on them . . . a spectacle that confounded the imagination, surpassing in grim horror anything we had ever seen before." Shown at the moment of firing are two 12-inch mortars in action. *U.S. Park Service*

hours before dark in order to approach Mindanao at dawn. Sighted an enemy destroyer at 15,000 yards but escaped unseen, making the scheduled run despite heavy seas and severe buffeting. Upon arrival at Mindanao we learned that of four planes dispatched only one had arrived and that without brakes or superchargers and being unfit for its mission it had already departed. Brett selected three more planes for the trip of which one developed mechanical trouble and two arrived safely taking the entire party out. Safe arrival and departure forced us to pass the latitude of Ambon at dawn but our course was set somewhat to the eastward enabling the party to escape interception. We landed at Batchellor Field while Darwin was under air raid."

Surrender in the Philippines

Despite overwhelming odds and under constant attack, MacArthur's troops on Bataan held on for roughly another two months after he left for Australia. Finally, in April 1942, when they had been reduced by hunger, disease, and casualties to the point of military helplessness, Major General Edward P. King, Jr., their commander, decided that he had no choice but to surrender. A description of that painful moment comes from a wartime report by the Provisional Tank Group: "At about 2230 General King announced to the three general officers present that further resistance would result in the massacres of the 6000 sick and wounded in the area and the 40,000 refugees now congested closely about; that he was out of touch with any troops that might be still resisting behind the closely drawn lines; that there were less than 25 percent effective of those now holding; that at most he could not hold more than the next day; that he was going to send a flag across the line at daylight; that he would take this action on his own responsibility. Asked by the tank commander if any help was in prospect, he answered negatively. Destruction of the main ordnance dumps was to commence at 2340. Troops would destroy their arms and equipment and cease resistance at 0700 the 9th."

U.S. Army Colonel Milton A. Hill (a veteran of the fighting for Bataan) described in a wartime article some of his impressions gleaned from the fall of Bataan: "Most American soldiers don't have much honest hate for the German or Jap until some of his comrades have been killed by the enemy, or until he himself has been made to suffer at the enemy's hands. This was true right on Bataan, and I say this without taking away one particle from the splendid fighting spirit I saw there or from the innumerable deeds of fighting craft and courage that were done there.

"But the Jap hates the American with a downright hate that carries him through in battle to success or death. And we could do with more of a similar individual fighting spirit. On Bataan our troops soon learned the usual lessons of battle—that it is a case of kill or be killed. And as I have said a lot of them [Americans] were killed or wounded because they had not had complete training in this basic idea of combat. They learned this lesson, but by no means all of them gained the spirit that goes beyond it—the belief in the heart of every man that he must kill the enemy, and the feelings that he wants to kill him to the extreme of his own fighting ability."

On Corregidor, the constant Japanese bombardment of the island was taking a heavy toll. From a wartime report comes this extract: "At this time, May 1-5, it became evident that surrender was just a question of time. Guns were being damaged and destroyed more rapidly than the Ordnance could repair them. Beach defense positions were being whittled away daily. The topography itself was being altered. The north shore road north of Malinta hill was literally blown into the Bay. Battery Commanders were reporting an increasing number of

shell shocked cases daily."

On May 5, 1942, the Japanese managed to land their troops on Corregidor. Despite heavy losses, the Japanese continued to funnel more troops plus tanks onto the island. On May 6, 1942, Lieutenant General Jonathan M. Wainwright, MacArthur's successor in the Philippines, surrendered the remainder of the American and Philippine forces to the local Japanese military commanders.

An American officer captured on Corregidor wrote in a report: "On 8 May, I was taken by a Japanese officer to tour the island. He was interested in knowing why Corregidor failed to capitulate with Bataan. He remarked that Corregidor's failure to surrender with Bataan caused them great inconvenience. To my question as to the size of the attacking force, he refused to answer. He admitted surprise at the resistance encountered—he said he did not expect to find any opposition. He admitted that two thirds of the landing barges leaving Bataan were sunk, but only fifty percent of the occupants were drowned. . . . I estimate the enemy lost 5,000 men killed or drowned, and 3,000 men wounded in the landing operation on Corregidor. Our

President Roosevelt had personally authorized Wainwright to decide if, or when, surrender was proper. Late on May 6, 1942, Wainwright broadcast a message to the Japanese asking for surrender terms. Wainwright tried to limit the surrender to his forces on Corregidor, but the Japanese insisted that surrender include all U.S. forces in the Philippine islands. Wainwright finally surrendered to the Japanese on May 8, 1942. Some American and Philippine units refused to surrender and fought on until about June 9, 1942. This Japanese wartime picture shows the surrender of the defenders of Corregidor. *MacArthur Memorial*

casualties were between 600 and 800 killed and about 1,000 wounded."

Besides the thousands of U.S. Army and Philippine Army soldiers who surrendered with the fall of Corregidor, there were also a large number of men from the other services that fell into Japanese hands. From a U.S. Navy communiqué of May 6, 1942, comes this extract: "When Corregidor fell, there were approximately 175 officers and 2,100 men of the Navy, and 70 officers and 1,500 men of the Marine Corps in the defending forces."

Summary

MacArthur's many mistakes in defending the Philippines are noted in the official U.S. Army history of World War II: "The decision to defend the whole island chain was questionable from a military standpoint. The United States was committed by mid-1941 to an Atlantic-first strategy and could not pour into the Philippines the resources required to make the islands secure. The prewar Plan ORANGE that called for a limited defense of the strongly fortified positions around Manila Bay was more in keeping with the global strategy adopted in 1941. MacArthur's ambitious plans and the defense measures that he and the War Department were able to put in place by December 8, 1941, had some value as a deterrent to Japanese aggression, but they were insufficient to meet an invasion when that deterrence failed.

"The most damaging effect of MacArthur's plan was the dispersal of supplies from the Bataan and Corregidor strongholds. Once the invasion came, the resulting chaos and the poor communications system made it impossible to re-create adequate depots to supply the fighting troops. Although the Philippine garrison held for just short of the planned six months, adequate supplies might have sustained a longer defense and would certainly have eased the suffering of the men on Bataan. Moreover, it is imperative to meet an invasion in the first critical hours before a beachhead is established, but MacArthur held his best troops, the Philippine Division, in reserve in the center of Luzon. The division was consequently unable to reach the landing sites in time to repulse the invaders, although it was in position to assist in the retreat to Bataan.

"The position of MacArthur's forces on the eve of battle suggests that he was in a sense trying to follow both his new defensive plan and Plan ORANGE. It could be argued that his orders combined the least compatible elements of both. But in the larger view, neither plan really held out any hope for defeating the Japanese aggressors. The fact that the campaign in the Philippines showed so clearly that the United States was unprepared for war in December 1941 was perhaps its most important lesson."

Chapter Two

MacArthur Goes On The Offensive

After the surrender of the Philippines, MacArthur sent President Roosevelt a message on May 8, 1942, describing his opinion of the threat now posed to Australia by Japanese military might: "I deem it of the utmost importance to provide adequate security for Australia and the Pacific Area, thus maintaining a constant frontal defense and a flank threat against further movement to the southward. This should be followed at the earliest possible moment by offensive action or at least by a sufficiently dangerous initial threat of offensive action to affect the enemy plans and dispositions. . . . The first step in the execution of this conception is the strengthening of the position in this area. At this time there are present all the elements to produce another disaster. If serious enemy pressure were applied against Australia prior to the development of adequate and balanced land, sea, and air forces, the situation would be extremely precarious. The extent of territory to be defended is so vast and the communication facilities are so poor that the enemy, moving freely by water, has a preponderant advantage . . ."

The immediate problem of the War Department was not only to enable MacArthur to build up in Australia a strong base of operations, but to man and defend the line of communications from the United States to Australia. This was critically important, for Australia was the last base of operations left to the Allies in the Southwest Pacific.

By March 1942, the Japanese had taken Singapore and overrun the Dutch East Indies. They were also beginning to threaten the line

MacArthur flew into Australia aboard a B-17 bomber on March 17, 1942. Pictured inside a B-17 bomber, MacArthur points out something of interest to the crew. Instead of facing a court-martial or being relieved of his command for the loss of the Philippines, MacArthur was seen by the American people as the "Hero of the Pacific." This strange turn of events had a lot to do with MacArthur's skill at cultivating the press, and his hard-working public relations staff. In the United States, MacArthur's powerful friends in the newspaper publishing business did much to help create the image of MacArthur as a heroic figure on a grand scale. *MacArthur Memorial*

Throughout the Japanese military campaign to seize the Philippines in 1941 and 1942, the dramatic and always inaccurate press releases from MacArthur's public relations staff in the Philippines had helped convince the American public that MacArthur alone was responsible for the Japanese failure at winning a quick and easy victory in the Philippines. Little or no mention was ever made of the common American or Philippine soldiers who slowed down the Japanese offensive with their blood and courage. Pictured in Australia is MacArthur and his chief of staff Major General Richard Sutherland. *MacArthur Memorial*

Shown in Australia is MacArthur conferring with General Sir Thomas Blamey, the top Australian military leader during World War II. General Dwight D. Eisenhower, MacArthur's former aide in the Philippines, was strongly against MacArthur being pulled out of the Philippines and given another command. Eisenhower believed that MacArthur was not competent to be given another command. President Roosevelt also had strong doubts about MacArthur's military skills. However, Roosevelt felt that he had to bow to both public opinion and political pressures and give MacArthur command of all Allied Forces in Australia. *MacArthur Memorial*

between the United States and Australia, pointing a drive into the Solomon Islands and toward Port Moresby, in New Guinea, from which they could threaten Australia itself.

The War Department threw every unit it could find, except token forces sent to Iceland and Northern Ireland, into strengthening the 6,000-mile line to Australia and building up the strength at MacArthur's disposal. Air bases were garrisoned along a string of islands from Hawaii to New Zealand, so that the Army Air Corps could help the Navy to keep the line open.

In agreement with the British, the Pacific Theater was made an area of United States strategic responsibility in the spring of 1942. Once the British had agreed that the Pacific Theater should be a U.S. responsibility and MacArthur had arrived in Australia, the Joint Chiefs of Staff, with the approval of President Roosevelt, on March 30, 1942, divided the theater into two major areas: the Southwest Pacific Area (SWPA) and the Pacific Ocean Areas. MacArthur was named supreme commander of the Southwest Pacific Area, which included Australia, New Guinea, the Philippine Islands, the South China Sea, the Gulf of Siam, and the Netherlands East Indies (except Sumatra). Admiral Chester W. Nimitz, who was already commanding the U.S. Navy Pacific Fleet, was named commander in chief of the Pacific Ocean Areas, which comprised the remainder of the Pacific Ocean west of the North American continent except for a small area off the western coast of Central and South America.

President Roosevelt and General George C. Marshall, head of the Joint Chiefs of Staff, had felt very strongly that a single supreme commander in charge of all naval, ground, and air units needed to be appointed in the Pacific Theater. Unfortunately, neither the Army or Navy would serve under the command of the other service. The results of this fierce inter-service rivalry led to each service getting its own pond to play in. Instead of a single major advance toward Japan, there would be two separate axis of advances. Instead of combining their military might together for the common cause of defeating Japan, each service would prove to be much more interested in improving its tainted reputation rather than working together. The Navy wanted to erase the embarrassment of Pearl Harbor while

President Roosevelt had hoped to name a single commander to manage the war in the Pacific against the Japanese, much like the role Eisenhower played in the war against Germany. However, the U.S. Navy strongly believed that the Pacific was peculiarly its province. The Navy's top admirals let Roosevelt know that they would never consent to placing the Pacific fleet under control of any Army officer, especially somebody they detested as much as MacArthur. Pictured together with President Roosevelt are MacArthur and Admiral Nimitz. *MacArthur Memorial*

MacArthur and the Army wanted to make up for their loss of the Philippines.

The First Offense

In the early summer of 1942, after the Battle of Midway, it became possible for the Allies to launch a limited offensive of their own to protect the line of communications and to prevent the Japanese from consolidating their gains. Accordingly, on July 2, 1942, the U.S. Joint Chiefs of Staff, the organization responsible for the direction of the war in the Pacific, issued orders that set in motion the first offensive of the Pacific war. Rabaul on the island of New Britain, the strategic hub of the Japanese line to Australia and the South Pacific and the bastion covering or flanking all approaches to the inner citadel of Japan's defense, was its goal.

Pictured in the Pacific is the U.S. Navy heavy cruiser the *Santa Fe*. Eighteen vessels of this type were built before World War II. The Navy's plan to push the Japanese military out of the Pacific was envisioned as a drive across the Central Pacific to the very doorstep of the Japanese home islands. The Navy used the Marine Corps to capture strategic islands that could be used as resupply points for the fleet. The Navy saw little need to recapture the Philippines in its grand plan. In the Navy's plans, the Army was seen only as a supporting force tasked with the job of guarding Pacific islands captured by the Marine Corps. *Real War Photos*

With its large harbor, numerous airfields, and natural defenses, Rabaul provided a sanctuary from which the Japanese could resupply their forces in the Solomon Islands, launch an assault on Australia, or threaten the vital supply lines linking Australia and the United States.

Rabaul as an objective was far beyond the capabilities of the meager forces available to the Allies in July 1942. Recognizing this fact, the Joint Chiefs of Staff specified that Rabaul would be taken in three stages: first, the seizure of bases in the southern Solomons; second, the reoccupation of the remainder of the Solomons and the north coast of New Guinea as far as Lae and Salamaua; and third, the recapture of Rabaul itself and the rest of the Bismarck Archipelago.

MacArthur voiced his own opinion to Washington about what plans should be used against the Japanese: "The first objective should be the New Britain New Ireland area, against which I would move immediately if the means were available . . . recommend 1 division trained and equipped for amphibious operations and a task force, including 2 carriers, be made available to me at earliest practicable date; with such a force I could retake that important area. . . . Speed is vital; not possible for me to act quickly if I must build equipment and train my divisions; cannot urge too strongly that the time has arrived to use the force, or a portion of it, which you have informed me to be 40,000 men on the west coast (U.S.A.) trained for amphibious operations, and could be employed in conjunction with the forces available to me in the initiation of offensive operations in the SWPA."

In laying the groundwork for the projected offensive in July, the Joint Chiefs gave the command of the South Pacific Area, and control over the first stage of the offensive, to Vice Admiral Robert L. Ghormley (after October 1942, Admiral Halsey). Ghormley would in turn be subordinate to Nimitz, who commanded the Pacific Ocean Areas. In his own area, Ghormley exercised unity of command over all the forces—sea, ground, and air. Strategic direction of the second and final phases of the offensive against Rabaul was assigned to both MacArthur and Nimitz by the Joint Chiefs. For themselves, the Joint Chiefs

The Joint Chiefs of Staff under the chairmanship of U.S. Army General George C. Marshall, shown here (right) with MacArthur, eventually came to an agreement in March 1942 with the Navy top brass in which the Pacific area of operations was divided into separate commands. MacArthur was appointed Supreme Commander (a title which he would change himself to Commander in Chief) of the Southwest Pacific Area. Admiral Chester W. Nimitz was placed in command of the rest of the Pacific. *MacArthur Memorial*

of Staff reserved control over the assignment of tasks, allocation of resources, and timing of operations in the two areas, thus exercising, in effect, some form of unified command over the entire Pacific Theater.

MacArthur wasn't happy about the command setup or the aims of the planned offensive. This can be seen in a June 24, 1942, message to Washington: "Impracticable to attempt the capture of Rabaul by direct assault supported by the amount of land-based aviation now available; my plan contemplates a progressive movement, involving primary action against the Solomons and the north coast of New Guinea, in order to protect the naval surface forces and to secure airfields from which

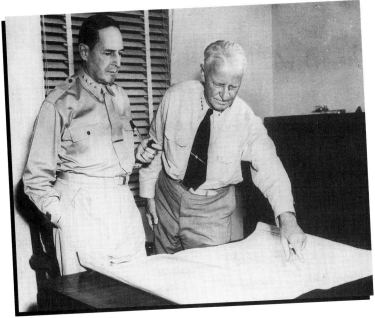

Encouraged by the Navy's victories at The Battle of the Coral Sea and Midway, MacArthur pushed both President Roosevelt and the Joint Chiefs of Staff to provide him with enough men and materiel to start him on the road back to the Philippines. MacArthur wanted to begin his campaign to retake the Philippines by assaulting the large Japanese naval base at Rabaul, on the island of New Britain. Pictured is MacArthur (left) explaining to Nimitz his plans for attacking Rabaul. *MacArthur Memorial*

land forces from other areas with a view to their operation under naval direction exercised from distant points can result in nothing but complete confusion; the very purpose of the establishment of the Southwest Pacific Area was to obtain unity of command. . . . If correct [command] procedure is not followed it makes a mockery of the unity of command theory, which was the basis of the organizational plan applied to the Pacific Theater."

Despite MacArthur's advice, the first offensive operation against the Japanese began on August 7, 1942, with the landing of a Marine division on the island of Guadalcanal. The fight for Guadalcanal was in doubt for almost three months, before the island was finally won in January 1943, with heavy losses on both sides. Now the Allies were firmly established in the Solomons, and the drive to encircle Rabaul could begin.

MacArthur's forces of the Southwest Pacific Area had meanwhile been forced by a Japanese drive toward Port Moresby (on the island of New Guinea) to begin an unplanned offensive of their own. In a message to Washington, MacArthur described this offensive: "This operation represents another phase in the pattern of the enemy's plans to capture Port Moresby. This citadel is guarded by the natural defense line of the Owen Stanley

essential support can be given to the forces participating in the final phase of the operation; necessary that all ground operations in this area be under my direction; to bring in

Unhappily for MacArthur, the Joint Chiefs of Staff decided that he didn't have the men and materiel to successfully assault the Japanese-held fortress of Rabaul on the island of New Britain. Pictured in this aerial shot are Japanese ships in the harbor of Rabaul on November 11, 1943. Instead of attacking Rabaul directly, it was decided to launch America's first ground offensive against the Japanese-held island of Guadalcanal. While the Navy and the Marines were tasked with the capture of Guadalcanal, MacArthur's forces were assigned the capture of locations along the southeast New Guinea coast in order to build airfields for land-based aircraft. *U.S. Navy*

Waiting for the Japanese to show themselves, these two American soldiers keep aim with their weapons. Fighting in the jungles of New Guinea, American soldiers found that the typical field of fire was often limited to no more then 5 to 10 yards. Jungle undergrowth could be so dense that clearing fire lanes around a defensive position could take up to a week. In such terrain, the maximum effective range of small arms fire was no more than 250 yards, even under the best conditions. *Real War Photos*

Range. The first effort was to turn its left flank from Lae and Salamaua which proved impracticable. He then launched an attack in large convoy force against its rear. This was repulsed and dissipated by air and sea action in the Coral Sea. He then tried to pierce the center in a weak attempt by way of Buna-Gona Kokoda subjecting himself to extraordinary air losses because of the extreme vulnerability of his exposed position. His latest effort was to turn the right flank by a surprise attack at Milne Bay. The move was anticipated, however, and prepared for with great care. With complete secrecy the position was occupied by our forces and converted into a strong point. The enemy fell into the trap with disastrous results to him."

In May 1942, the Japanese had been thwarted in the Battle of the Coral Sea from taking Port Moresby by sea. In August the Japanese had begun pushing overland across the towering Owen Stanley Mountains of New Guinea toward Port Moresby from the northeastern coast of the island. By mid-September they were within 20 miles of their objective. MacArthur now had to commit strong Australian units to push the Japanese back to the north coast in an operation known as the Papuan campaign. Mid-November found the

Crossing a makeshift jungle bridge, these American soldiers head deeper into the New Guinea jungle. Combat in New Guinea showed MacArthur's troops that the direction of a Japanese infantry attack could shift completely during a combat engagement due to the cover provided by dense jungle growth. It was also discovered that a Japanese attacker could pass within 5 yards of an American soldier without either knowing the other was near. In many jungle encounters, both sides were often forced to reverse directions to continue the battle since neither side could find the other among the undergrowth. *Real War Photos*

Japanese firmly entrenched in the Buna-Gona region of New Guinea where, as at Guadalcanal, the enemy received reinforcements from the Japanese stronghold of Rabaul. The Japanese clung desperately to their positions in New Guinea. It took almost three months and the combined efforts of two Australian divisions, a U.S. Army division, and another U.S.

Envisioned by American military leaders as missions that could be completed in a few weeks, both the campaign to capture Guadalcanal and MacArthur's endeavors in New Guinea took months of hard fighting to resolve. On the lookout for a Japanese attack, these American soldiers keep their weapons at the ready. In the jungles of New Guinea, MacArthur's soldiers found themselves fighting two enemies: man and nature. Of the two, nature was often the more formidable. *Real War Photos*

Army regiment to clear the Japanese from the Buna-Gona area of New Guinea.

The Green Hell

From a wartime article in *Yank* magazine come these extracts describing combat conditions in the jungles of New Guinea by an anonymous American soldier: "We were over the Owen Stanley range to relieve an Australian combat unit, which was keeping open a trail over which natives were bringing up supplies. . . . The lieutenant sent back for me to bring my squad forward and relieve the right squad. Because so many of the squad had been killed and wounded or had passed out from heat exhaustion, I thought I might find a better place to put my men. So I crawled forward to find positions for them. I had found a few good shell holes, some logs, and depressions in the ground, when a .30-caliber machine gun opened fire on me. The first burst hit the front handle grip of my Tommy gun, and, of course, I got as low as possible; but the second burst hit my Tommy gun drum, and two bullets hit me in the arm. Also, fragments of the drum hit me hard on the hand and shoulder. These .30's were explosive bullets which broke up my arm and tore a great deal of flesh away from it. It felt as if an ax blade was shearing through the flesh of my arm. . . . Just as I was getting in the right position to shoot, a .25-caliber machine gun opened up from the left. One bullet hit me in the elbow and one in the ribs—the latter went through my pipe and a can of tobacco and only broke my rib. I pulled out this bullet myself, burning my index finger on the hot lead. Another bullet went through my helmet and just grazed my scalp.

"I lay there for about 3 hours in the hot sun, bleeding profusely. Figuring that I would bleed to death if I remained there, I began to crawl back to my own men—only hoping and trusting to God that he would give me strength and protection to get back. I got back to my men, and the platoon medical personnel made a hasty cross splint and sling for my mangled left arm.

"One of my men helped me back to the command post where litter bearers took me back to a dispensary. Attendants gave me morphine and put me on a jeep, which carried me

Jumping out of truck, a Japanese Army squad prepares to enter combat. The standard Japanese military rifle during World War II was the old-fashioned bolt-action Ariska. Reasonably accurate up to 600 yards with only a very slight recoil, the weapon weighed 10 pounds, 2 ounces, including bayonet. The Japanese soldier considered the bayonet an essential weapon. Almost invariably, wartime pictures show the Japanese soldier carrying his rifle with the bayonet fixed. The bayonet itself was 15 1/2 inches long. *Author's collection*

back—with several other casualties—to a portable hospital. There medical officers removed two bullets. Next day I was sent to a landing field where a plane was waiting to take casualties to Port Moresby."

American Military Shortcomings

MacArthur's Papuan (New Guinea) campaign to protect and later drive the Japanese away from Port Moresby had started in late July 1942 and had lasted until January 23, 1943. While ultimately successful, the campaign showed that the U.S. Army had some serious training deficiencies. American soldiers were poorly led, insufficiently hardened for extended forced marches, poorly schooled in the techniques of night patrolling and assaulting Japanese defensive positions, and generally unprepared for operations in a tropical environment.

A U.S. Army infantry officer whose unit had already seen combat in the jungle was asked what he would do if he could train his men again. He stated: "I would have some maneuvers on which the men were deprived

To back up their field mortars, Japanese infantry units were provided with the Type 92 70-mm Battalion gun (howitzer) such as this one being fired by American soldiers on Saipan. Every Japanese infantry battalion had at least two of these small, short-barreled weapons. Weighing 468 pounds, the Type 92 could fire an 8.3-pound high-explosive round about 2 miles. In the jungle, this weapon could be broken down into a number of components that could be transported by either animal transport or on the backs of Japanese soldiers. *U.S. Marine Corps*

To support their infantry soldiers in battle, the Japanese deployed a large number of infantry mortars ranging in size from 50mm up to 250mm. The standard medium-range Japanese mortar was the 81-mm Type 99 as pictured here in a privately-owned military museum in Northern California. Weighing in at about 52 pounds, this crew-served weapon could fire a 7-pound high-explosive round up to a distance of 2,000 yards. *Michael Green*

of sleep, food, water and comforts in order to find out which noncoms and men can't take it. I would then relieve these particular ones. This type of maneuver would teach men to know and expect hardships. It will lessen the shock when they come up against the real thing in the presence of the enemy."

MacArthur's ground forces also failed to make much use of their artillery and instead depended on close-air support to blast away Japanese defensive positions. When weather or other factors prevented the use of aircraft the ground forces took heavy losses in missions that could have been easily achieved with artillery fire with little or no loss of life for the infantry. Even when air support was available, it was often poorly coordinated with ground units. Not only did aircraft bomb their own units several times, they also on occasion missed targets entirely.

Tanks which could have greatly aided MacArthur's forces in overcoming well-prepared Japanese defensive positions were not brought into operation until the very closing stages of the campaign.

The inability of MacArthur's support formations to maintain a steady stream of supplies to the front-line combat formations during the campaign seriously damaged troop morale, already threatened by the hostile climate of the area. American soldiers fighting the Japanese in the jungle hell of New Guinea found themselves short of food, water, ammunition, and medicine. One of MacArthur's infantry divisions, with a total strength of almost 11,000 men before the campaign lost over 7,000 men to various illnesses. Total combat losses for the Papuan campaign were 8,546 killed and wounded.

The Fight Continues

After the Papuan and Guadalcanal campaigns there was a five-month lull while Admiral Halsey, now commander of the South Pacific Area, and General MacArthur gathered resources and prepared bases for the second phase of the drive toward Rabaul.

This is not to say there were no operations during this period. The Japanese made a major effort to reinforce their position in the Solomons and New Guinea. Their attempt in

A bit larger than the Type 92 70-mm Battalion gun was the Japanese 75-mm Meiji 41 Regimental gun (howitzer). Like the Type 92 gun, the 75-mm Meiji 41 gun could be broken down into a number of components to allow the weapons to be carried by animal or human transport. Pictured are Japanese soldiers carrying up a steep hill the various components that make up a Type 92 gun. Weighing 1,200 pounds, the Meiji 41 gun could hurl a 14-pound high-explosive shell about 4 miles. *Author's collection*

Comparable to the Japanese Meiji 41 gun was the American World War II M116 75-mm Pack Howitzer pictured in use here. Developed before World War II, the M116 weighed about 653 pounds. With a crew of four, the howitzer could throw a 14-pound shell almost 6 miles. Like the Japanese gun, the M116 was designed to be broken down into a number of components that could be carried by animal transport or packed into a large crate that could be dropped by parachute. Because of its weight, the M116 was used extensively by the American military throughout the Pacific campaigns. *U.S. Army*

One size larger than the M116 75-mm Pack howitzer in the American military inventory was the M3 105-mm howitzer, one of which is shown firing at a Japanese pillbox. Not a complete success in service, the M3 was basically a cut-down version of the Army's standard 105-mm howitzer mounted on the gun mount of the M116 howitzer. Weighing 2,500 pounds, the short-barreled M3 weighed about a ton less than the Army's standard 105-mm howitzer. *U.S. Army*

reduced the capabilities of the Japanese Combined Fleet, whose commander, Admiral Yamamoto, was shot down over Bougainville.

The second stages of the Allied offensive against Rabaul began in late June 1943 with the landings by forces from MacArthur's area on islands off eastern New Guinea and on the New Guinea coast northwest of Buna. At about the same time, Admiral Halsey's South Pacific forces, now operating under MacArthur's strategic direction, landed on New Georgia in the central Solomons. All of these operations were designed to secure air bases to support further advances in a two-pronged drive up the Solomons and the New Guinea coast toward Rabaul.

From a *Yank* magazine comes this excerpt from an article by Sgt. Mark Morriss: "With U.S. Occupational Forces on New Georgia—Hastings Ridge is just a little place, a sort of quiver in the convulsions of New Georgia's terrain.

"If the rough coral slopes were leveled and the steel-scarred trees were cleared away, there might be room for a football field, certainly nothing larger.

"Yet the Ridge was literally crawling with Japs—one machine gun company and one rifle company at least. For five days the Infantry attacked it and when they gained a foothold, they fought all day and all night and then the next day to hold it.

March 1943 to send a large convoy to Lee in New Guinea resulted in the Battle of the Bismarck Sea and the loss of over 3,500 men and many valuable ships. The following month Rabaul-based aircraft, reinforced by carrier planes from Truk, sought to knock out Allied air power in the Solomons, but to no avail. The loss of the carrier planes and pilots further

Developed in the United States during the 1930s, the M2 105-mm howitzer as shown here proved to be the mainstay of America's artillery inventory throughout World War II. With a firing crew of eight men, the M2 howitzer could fire a variety of different rounds (high-explosive, smoke, illuminated, gas) up to 10 miles at the rate of up to 8 rounds per minute. Due to the weapon's weight of 2,258 pounds, it was usually brought into action by truck. M2 105-mm howitzers were also mounted on halftracks and fully-tracked chassis during World War II. *Real War Photos*

"In the jungle, war is always a personal sort of thing, one man against another. On Hastings Ridge, it reached a point where individual action and individual courage were knitted together in two and three man units of assault, pitted against similar little units of Japs crouched in pillboxes. And the best fighters won because they cooperated with each other best.

"On the first day S/Sgt. Clarence Terry of Arco, Idaho, worked his platoon up the Ridge. Two of his sergeants were ahead of him, almost on top of a Jap pillbox, working together as a team. They were using grenades and rifles, and when Sgt. Roberts Chambers of Bend, Oreg., ran out of grenades, he called for his buddy to throw him more. The other sergeant tossed them forward and as he did a Jap rifleman in the pillbox shot him through

the chest. The sergeant was on his feet, and when the bullet bit into him he wheeled to face the Jap and yelled like a man fouled in a fist fight: 'Why, you dirty little bastard!' He raised his rifle, started forward and fell dead.

"Chambers, a few feet away, went blind mad. He hurled two grenades into the Jap position as though he was stoning a snake, then leaped into the pillbox with his trench knife. When he came out, he crouched over his teammate but there was no heartbeat; he had done all he could."

The campaign on New Guinea (from January 24, 1943, until December 1944) is all but forgotten except by those who served there. Battles with names like Tarawa, Saipan, and Iwo Jima overshadow it. Yet Allied operations in New Guinea were essential to the U.S. Navy's drive across the Central Pacific and to the U.S. Army's liberation of the Philippine Islands from Japanese occupation. The Allied advance along the northern New Guinea coastline toward the Philippines forced the Japanese to divert precious ships, planes, and men who might otherwise have reinforced their crumbling Central Pacific front.

The World's Worst Battlefield

New Guinea was not an easy place to wage war. It is the second-largest island in the world. Its northern coastline extends nearly 1,600 miles. A major mountain range cuts across the island's center from the eastern end of New Guinea to Geelvink Bay on the west and makes passage overland through the jungle mountains by large units nearly impossible. The lee of the mountainous spine, around the Port Moresby area, is wet from January to April but otherwise dry. On the windward side, scene of most of the ground fighting during 1942-1945, rainfall runs as high as 300 inches per year. As one veteran

After many of the battles in the Southwest Pacific Area were completed, American officers found that one of their biggest problems was trying to control the crowds of rear area support troops who wanted to see both the now-empty battlefields as well as look for souvenirs. If not stopped by military policemen, American soldiers would come off the battlefield with everything from flags to Chevrolet trucks. Pictured are American soldiers using a captured Japanese jeep to remove a wounded soldier from the battlefield. *Real War Photos*

recalled, "It rains daily for nine months and then the monsoon starts."

Disease thrived on New Guinea. Malaria was the greatest debilitation, but dengue fever, dysentery, scrub typhus, and a host of other tropical sicknesses awaited unwary soldiers in the jungle. Scattered, tiny coastal settlements dotted the flat malarial north coastline, but inland the lush tropical jungle swallowed men and equipment.

The terrain was a commander's nightmare because it fragmented the deployment of large formations. On the north shore a tangled morass of large mangrove swamps slowed overland movement. Monsoon rains of 8 or 10 inches a day turned torpid streams into impassable rivers. There were no roads or railways, and supply lines were often native tracks, usually a dirt trail a yard or so wide, tramped out over the centuries through the jungle growth. Downpours quickly dissolved such footpaths into calf-deep mud

Lying where they fell in battle are Japanese soldiers. American desire for Japanese military souvenirs was so great that some soldiers, Marines, and sailors starting collecting Japanese skulls from those killed in combat. Other items, from gold teeth to various bones, were also collected from Japanese corpses by American military personnel. This problem became so bad that in September 1942, the Navy issued orders that promised stern disciplinary action for anybody found tampering with Japanese corpses. *Real War Photos*

Pictured in the hands of these U.S. Marines is the American-designed and -built M1 rifle, commonly referred to as the "Garand" after its designer, John C. Garand. Most American soldiers fighting in the jungles of the Southwest Pacific felt that the M1 Garand rifle was far superior to anything used by the Japanese soldiers. Despite the power of the M1 Garand rifle, bullets from the Garand sometimes traveled only 100 to 200 feet before being stopped in a large tree, or by heavy jungle grass. *Real War Photos*

A favorite weapon among American soldiers fighting in the jungles of the Southwest Pacific was the Browning automatic rifle (BAR), as shown here in the arms of the soldier on the left in the picture. Despite the fact that a U.S. Army ten-man infantry squad is supposed to have only one BAR, many American soldiers fighting in the jungles of New Guinea would beg, steal, or borrow another BAR to beef up their squad's firepower with two or more BARs. For these soldiers, the difficulties encountered in traversing rough terrain with an extra BAR and ammunition were more than offset by the greater firepower they had when needed. *Real War Photos*

that reduced soldiers to exhausted automatons stumbling over the glue-like ground. Fed by the frequent downpours, the lush rain-forest jungle afforded excellent concealment for stubborn defenders and made coordinated overland attacks nearly impossible. Infantrymen carrying 60 pounds of weapons, equipment, and pack staggered along in temperatures reaching the mid-90s with humidity levels to match. Thus the U.S. Army faced a determined Japanese foe on a battleground riddled with disease and whose terrain made a mockery of standard military tactics.

From the official U.S. Army history of World War II come these excerpts describing the difficulties in supplying American troops fighting on New Guinea: "On 23 April heavy rains started to turn the road into a quagmire through which struggling men could scarcely carry their own equipment and food, to say nothing of extra supplies for the leading battalion . . . efforts at local air supply proved inadequate, and with no marked improvement of road conditions the supply situation for

A typical Japanese attack began with the infiltration of some of their men into American lines under cover of the night and jungle undergrowth. The Japanese also used the cover of darkness to set up their own supporting weapons, like machine guns and mortars, as close to the American positions as possible. Unfortunately, the poor level of noise discipline among some Japanese units often gave their positions away. It was at this point that American troops used their mortars to plaster Japanese positions and break up the attack before it could get started. Shown here is a detachment of U.S. Army 4.2-inch heavy mortars in action in the Pacific. *Real War Photos*

This prewar picture shows an American soldier demonstrating the proper way to throw a hand grenade. During the fighting in the Southwest Pacific, U.S. soldiers had a variety of hand grenades to use against the Japanese. These included white smoke grenades, white phosphorus grenades, incendiary grenades, and colored grenades. The most common grenade used by U.S. soldiers in World War II was the Mark II A1 fragmentation hand grenade. Copied from a World War I French grenade design, the Mark II consisted of a serrated, cast-iron body filled with TNT. *U.S. Park Service*

American antiaircraft units played a very important role in MacArthur's campaigns in the Pacific during World War II. Antiaircraft guns protected airfields, supply depots, and beachhead positions from Japanese warplanes. The range of weapons employed by American antiaircraft units included everything from .50-caliber machine guns up to radar-directed 90-mm guns. Pictured here is a .50-caliber (water-cooled) Browning M3 machine gun. *Real War Photos*

In the jungles of New Guinea, American soldiers found that their old bolt-action M1903A3 Springfield rifles operated longer than the semi-automatic M1 Garand. This was because you could force the bolt into place on a Springfield rifle when it was jammed up with mud or grime. You couldn't do this with a Garand because of its more-complex firing mechanism. Pictured are American soldiers on patrol in the dense jungle growth of New Guinea. *Real War Photos*

troops inland deteriorated rapidly. The 186th Infantry, for instance, subsisted for three or four days principally on rice and canned fish from a captured Japanese ration dump."

MacArthur sent a message to Washington describing what his men were going through on New Guinea: "For more than three weeks during that period, every unit forced its way through deep forests and ravines, and climbed scores of peaks in pursuit of the enemy. Traversing knee deep mud, clambering up steep precipices, bearing uncomplainingly the heavy weight of artillery ammunition, our men overcame the shortage of our supplies, and

we succeeded in surmounting the Stanley Range. No pen or word can depict adequately the magnitude of the hardships suffered. From the bottom of our hearts we appreciate these many hardships and deeply sympathize with the great numbers killed and wounded."

The major objective of the offensive operations conducted on New Guinea was to acquire airfields from which MacArthur's land-based planes could support future operations in the Southwest Pacific Area. MacArthur knew that the key to any successful operation against the Japanese was local command of both the air and sea.

The best-known antiaircraft gun used by American military forces in the Pacific during World War II was the Swedish-designed 40-mm Borfor gun, which was adopted into both U.S. Navy and Army service shortly before Pearl Harbor. In Army service, the Borfor gun was mounted on a simple four-wheel towed carriage. In this configuration, the weapon was air-cooled. In U.S. Navy service, the Borfor was normally mounted in twin-gun water-cooled mounts designed for more sustained use than its ground counterpart. *Real War Photos*

The most powerful antiaircraft gun employed by the American Army in the Pacific during World War II was the 90-mm gun, as pictured here with its crew. This type of weapon was also used by MacArthur's troops in both direct and indirect modes as artillery during the fight for the main island of Luzon in the Philippines. American-built 90-mm antiaircraft guns were credited with 75 Japanese cave positions closed, 40 pillboxes destroyed, 25 gun positions knocked out, and 7 Japanese machine gun nests destroyed. *Real War Photos*

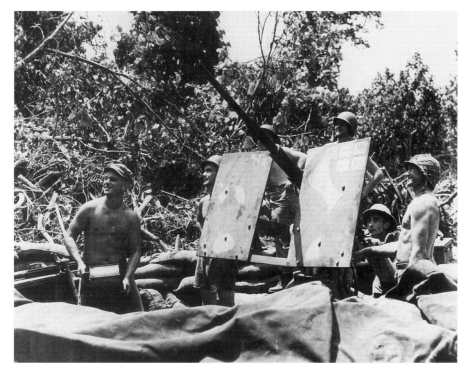

Normally mounted only on U.S. Navy ships, this Swiss-designed Oerlikon 20-mm antiaircraft machine gun and its entire naval mount has been moved ashore to guard an island airfield from air attack by the Japanese. Manned by a Marine in this picture, the Oerlikon had a 280-round-per-minute rate of fire and a 2,000-yard effective range. The Marine Corps also modified a small number of older, 37-mm antiaircraft gun mounts into twin mounts for the much more effective 20-mm Oerlikon guns during World War II. *Real War Photos*

Naval and air forces were of major importance in the offensive: the navy to transport invading forces, protect their advance and supply lines from sea attacks, and help reduce enemy coastal defenses; the air force to cover the amphibious attacks, neutralize enemy air power, and cooperate in the ground operations.

Despite the importance of air power in the Pacific war, MacArthur never had the full support of fast carrier forces used so effectively in the Central Pacific. Most of MacArthur's military campaigns were limited by the range of his land-based aircraft.

MacArthur was never a big fan of the U.S. Navy (and they weren't crazy about him either), and the lack of naval air support during these campaigns caused him to send a message to Washington which clearly expressed his anger: "My own operations in New Guinea have been supported only by short-range aircraft. My operation to capture the north coast of New Guinea in full swing; am greatly hampered by the total lack of light shipping, landing boats, and barges, which I have previously requested; in their absence am moving overland and by air; supply is the controlling factor and must be accomplished by native carrier and by air; improvised landing fields have been and are being prepared. . . . Supply difficulties

incredible and limit speed of movement and size of forces and are of course multiplied by lack of shipping and shortage of transport planes; the possibility of success of the movement and the time factor are still unpredictable; under severe pressure from this Headquarters, much progress has been made beginning with the development of Port Moresby, which had initially a garrison of a regiment of militia, one landing strip without parking space for planes and a port capacity of only 500 tons a day.

"If we are defeated in the Solomons, as we must be unless the Navy accepts successfully the challenge of the enemy surface fleet, the entire Southwest Pacific Area will be in the gravest danger; information derived from enemy sources indicates that an attack on Milne Bay and possibly elsewhere in New Guinea is contemplated for mid-November; urge that the entire resources of the United States be used temporarily to meet the critical situation that shipping be made available from any source, that one corps be dispatched immediately; that all available heavy bombers be ferried here at once and that urgent action be taken to increase the air strength at least to the full complement allotted for this area; that immediate action be taken to prepare bases for

An important aircraft in the Southwest Pacific Area was the four-engine B-17 bomber. The aircraft's long range and heavy bomb load was much appreciated by American soldiers fighting in New Guinea. Unfortunately, interservice rivalries reared their ugly heads over the employment of the B-17 bomber in the Southwest Pacific. The U.S. Navy complained that MacArthur was using his B-17s primarily against Japanese airfields instead of enemy shipping as the Navy wanted. Pictured in Europe is a B-17E model. *Real War Photos*

naval operations on the east coast of Australia; that the British Eastern Fleet be moved to the west coast of Australia."

The Japanese strongly defended New Georgia and Bougainville. The Munda airfield on New Georgia was finally captured in August 1943, but the island group was not secured until October. On November 1, 1943, Bougainville was invaded. But not until late-November 1943 was the beachhead at Empress Augusta Bay secured.

The Japanese took extreme risks to meet the dangerous challenges of the Allies in the air

and on the sea. For example, to reinforce Rabaul, they sent in 173 planes from the Combined Fleet and based them at Truk and thereby immobilized their fleet. During November and part of December 1943, Japanese planes from Rabaul attacked the Allied beachhead at Bougainville day and night, struck at Allied convoys, and engaged Allied fighters repeatedly. The results were slim—three Allied ships damaged, one sunk—hardly worth the prices of more than 129 carrier aircraft and 70 other planes the Japanese had to pay. These losses, together with damages inflicted on Japanese heavy cruisers by

Allied air attacks against Rabaul, crippled the Japanese Combined Fleet and had a vital effect on the balances of naval power in the Central Pacific for the rest of the war.

With the development of an Allied air base on Bougainville, ground-based fighters and bombers began to strike at Rabaul in December 1943, thereby virtually assuring Allied success in the Solomons.

MacArthur sent a message to Washington in January 1944, describing the lessons learned from the fighting in the Solomons: "The destruction of the remnants of the enemy forces in the Sanananda area concludes the Papuan campaign. The Horii Army has been annihilated. The outstanding military lesson of this campaign was the continuous calculated application of air power, inherent in the potentialities of every component of the Air Forces, employed in the most intimate tactical and logistical union with ground troops. The effect of this modern instrumentality was sharply accentuated by the geographical limitations of this theater. For months on end, air transport with constant fighter coverage moved complete infantry regiments and artillery battalions across the almost impenetrable mountains and jungles of Papua, and the reaches of the sea; transported field hospitals and other base installations to the front, supplied the troops and evacuated casualties. For hundreds of miles bombers provided all-around reconnaissance, protected the coast from hostile naval intervention, and blasted the way for the infantry as it drove forward. A new form of campaign was tested

Shown here is an American wartime submarine's main control room. Peering through his periscope while looking for enemy ships is the submarine's commander. American submarines took a heavy toll on Japanese shipping during World War II. In 1942, a problem developed between MacArthur and Nimitz, who wanted to transfer some of MacArthur's subs to the South Pacific command. Despite MacArthur's refusal to hand over control of any of the subs under his command, the Joint Chiefs of Staff transferred twelve of his subs to the South Pacific command area anyway. *Real War Photos*

In a somewhat informal view of MacArthur, we see him chatting with Australian troops somewhere in New Guinea in 1943. The Japanese were not standing still in early 1943. Determined to retain control of Rabaul at all cost, the Japanese spared no effort to strengthen their bases in the Solomons and New Guinea. The Japanese Army felt that New Guinea was more important to defend since it was vital to the defense of the Philippines and the Dutch East Indies. New Guinea was also more suitable for large-scale Army operations than the smaller islands of the Solomons. *MacArthur Memorial*

which points the way to the ultimate defeat of the enemy in the Pacific."

Southwest Pacific forces meanwhile were pushing forward on the other prong of the offensive by way of New Guinea and Western New Britain. On New Guinea, Australian soldiers were called upon to do most of the dirty and dangerous work of rooting the Japanese out of their jungle hideaways. By mid-September 1943 Australian troops took Lae and Salamaua on the Huon Gulf opposite New Britain. They did this with the help of American Army paratroopers dropped behind them on an inland airfield. This was the first American airborne operation in the Pacific war. MacArthur had hoped to trap the Japanese on the Huon Peninsula, but they escaped to points farther west on the New Guinea coast before his invading force, which now included an American infantry division, secured this stepping stone in January 1944. The forces of both the South and Southwest Pacific were now in position before the Bismarck Barrier, ready for their final assault on Rabaul.

Pictured here is what's left of a Japanese destroyer after American firepower was finished with it. In early 1943, the Japanese Navy felt very strongly that they wished to concentrate their forces on defending the Solomons' approach to their large naval base at Rabaul. The Japanese Navy believed that the Solomon Islands offered good sites for naval bases and lent themselves to operations for which the Navy was best suited. Much to the dismay of the Japanese Navy, the Imperial General Headquarters in Tokyo decided it was more important to build up the defenses of New Guinea. *Real War Photos*

Pictured aboard his personal aircraft sometime in 1943, MacArthur appears deep in thought. By the spring of 1943, the Joint Chiefs had decided to continue their offensive in the South and Southwest Pacific Areas of operations. MacArthur and his Navy counterpart, Admiral William Halsey, came up with a plan codenamed "Cartwheel." Consisting of 13 separate operations to be completed in a period of eight months, Operation Cartwheel involved both air and ground forces from the Southwest and South Pacific Areas of command advancing by successive stages so that they could both converge on the Japanese stronghold of Rabaul. *MacArthur Memorial*

The first phase of MacArthur's and Halsey's Operation Cartwheel began on the last day of June 1943. Initial operations went fairly well. However, by August 1943, many top American military leaders started to have doubts about the necessity for actually trying to capture the heavily defended Japanese base at Rabaul. Typical of the types of weapon the Japanese had installed in large numbers at Rabaul to defend it from a possible American assault is this 120-mm coast artillery gun. *U.S. Marine Corps*

Shown in this wartime aerial picture is a Japanese Navy heavy cruiser suffering a direct hit while inside Rabaul Harbor. Despite the heavy losses in men and equipment that resulted in trying to capture Rabaul, MacArthur believed very strongly that the capture of Rabaul was needed before he could continue his advance up the New Guinea coast and then on to the Philippines. The Joint Chiefs disagreed with MacArthur's plans. Instead, they decided that the U.S. Navy's plan to advance on Japan from the Central Pacific made more sense and became the main effort in the Pacific. *U.S. Navy*

In January 1944, Australian soldiers fighting in New Guinea found a complete set of Japanese Army secret codes books. This incredible bit of good fortune would allow Mac-Arthur and his top commanders important insights on Japanese Army activities and plans in the Pacific area of operations for the rest of the war.

Despite the valuable information provided by the breaking of the Japanese Army codes and the great advantage that this provided MacArthur in planning his campaigns, MacArthur tended to ignore the information supplied to him by his code-breakers if it conflicted with his own grand plans to liberate the Philippines. Many an American soldier would die or be wounded in unnecessary battles that could have been avoided if MacArthur had paid more attention to his own intelligence sources.

Closing In on Rabaul

Before final operations against Rabaul itself began, the Joint Chiefs changed their plans. The seizure of the Japanese stronghold, they decided, would be too costly and would require such large resources as to delay the progress of the war in the Pacific unnecessarily. The same results could be obtained, they thought, by encircling Rabaul and neutralizing it by aerial bombardment and by seizing a strong base for their own use in the Admiralties. The Joint Chiefs therefore altered the objectives of the third and final phase of the New Guinea-Solomons offensive and revised the schedules of operations then in effect.

The first of these operations, the seizure of western New Britain, began on December 15, 1943, when MacArthur landed some of his forces on the opposite end of the island from the Japanese stronghold of Rabaul. MacArthur assigned General Walter Krueger's Sixth Army the task of taking the Arawe peninsula, which had a small harbor that would facilitate control of Vitiaz and Dampier straits, both of which separate New Guinea and the island of New Britain. General Krueger selected the 112th Cavalry Regiment, plus artillery, engineers, and other supporting forces to conduct the amphibious landings on the Arawe peninsula. The 112th Cavalry Regiment had only been stripped of its horses at the beginning of 1943. It had little or no training in the art of amphibious assault landings.

Despite intelligence reports that MacArthur's forces would meet only light Japanese resistance, the men of the 112th Cavalry Regiment ran into heavy enemy machine gun fire as they approached their landing points. Fortunately, the American superiority in firepower forced the numerically inferior Japanese to retreat. By the mid-afternoon of December 15th, MacArthur's forces had established a foothold on the western tip of the island of New Britain.

The Japanese, however, would not concede defeat. On the afternoon of December 15th, the Japanese began a series of furious air attacks that lasted several days on the American ships supporting the landing. In addition, the Japanese began bringing up infantry reinforcements which were dug-in just outside the American beachhead positions. To break through these newly dug-in Japanese defensive positions, Krueger decided to reinforce the 112th Cavalry Regiment with a Marine Corps tank company

and additional infantry. Using the armor-protected firepower of the Marine tanks, the American soldiers forced the Japanese from their trenches on January 16, 1944. The victory had been won at a cost of 118 Americans killed, 352 wounded, and 4 missing.

While the fighting for the Arawe peninsula was under way, Krueger decided to seize the

Pictured in early 1944 are MacArthur and Major General Horace H. Fuller walking along a New Guinea beach during the Hollandia invasion. Once the decision was made by the Joint Chiefs that the main advance to Japan would go through the Central Pacific under Nimitz's control, MacArthur feared that his Southwest Pacific Area of operations would become only a holding operation. MacArthur was assured by the Joint Chiefs that his operation would not be curtailed. MacArthur was told to complete Operation Cartwheel and his advance along the northeast coast of New Guinea. *MacArthur Memorial*

With a grenade going off in a Japanese dugout, American soldiers stand ready to fire at any enemy soldiers who attempt to escape. When Operation Cartwheel ended in early 1944, the Joint Chiefs of Staff gave MacArthur the go-ahead to plan an assault on the Philippines. Whatever pleasure MacArthur received by this news was tempered by the fact that the Joint Chiefs also told Nimitz to begin moving his forces toward the Philippines. *Real War Photos*

Pictured on a naval landing craft in early 1944 is MacArthur with his acting aide at the time, Colonel Lloyd Lehrabes. With the successful completion of Operation Cartwheel by MacArthur's and Halsey's forces in early 1944, the Japanese fortress at Rabaul was effectively cut off from resupply and left to wither on the vine for the rest of the war. The Japanese military efforts to prevent Rabaul from being captured or cut off had cost them dearly in ships, planes, and men. *MacArthur Memorial*

Japanese airfield at Cape Gloucester (also located on the western tip of New Britain). He gave this mission to the 1st Marine Division, veterans of the battle for Guadalcanal. Because the Japanese defenders had set up most of their defensive positions around the airfield, Krueger landed the Marines on an undefended beach about six miles away from the airfield. Advancing on the Japanese-held airfield the Marines, to their surprise, found the Japanese resistance was very light.

The bloodiest fighting for the Cape Gloucester area came when the Marines attempted to clear the jungles on the eastern side of their newly won airfield. The worst fighting came on January 1, 1944, along a stream later dubbed Suicide Creek. The Japanese soldiers had built a well-camouflaged bunker complex along the stream bank and succeeded in throwing back the attacking Marines for two days with heavy losses. Finally, Army engineers built a log road through the jungle so that American tanks could be brought up to point-blank range to blast the Japanese soldiers out of their bunkers.

In mid-February 1944, Halsey's New Zealand troops went into action to take an air base on Green Island, east of Rabaul, and on the last day of the month MacArthur's troops further tightened the circles by landing in the Admiralty Islands. This operation, undertaken initially as a reconnaissance in force, ultimately involved a full Army division.

For MacArthur, the seizure of the Admiralty Islands was very important from a tactical standpoint. The islands were only 200 miles northeast of Rabaul. Their capture would complete the surrounding of the Japanese stronghold.

MacArthur's amphibious landings were not always easy for the troops assigned the actual task of assaulting enemy beaches. From a wartime report by a *Yank* correspondent comes this vivid description of being in a small navy landing craft headed toward hostile shores: "As we neared the channel, the Navy men in the bow hollered to us to keep our heads down or we'd get them blown off. We crouched lower, swearing, and waiting. It came with a crack; machine gun fire over our heads. Our light landing craft shuddered as the Navy gunners hammered back and answered with the .30 calibers mounted on both sides of the barge. As we made the turn for the beach, something solid plugged into us. 'They got one of our guns or something,' one GI said. There was a splinter the size of a half dollar on the pack of the man in front of me. Up front a hole gaped in

Pictured shaking hands with MacArthur is Major General Frederick A. Irving, commander of the 24th Infantry Division during the invasion of the Hollandia-Aitape area of New Guinea in April 1944. The seizure of this area of New Guinea, on the northeast coast of the island, was important to MacArthur since it was a first step in his planned invasion of the Philippines. Anchorages at Hollandia were capable of basing many of MacArthur's largest combat vessels, cargo ships, and troop transports. *MacArthur Memorial*

the middle of the landing ramp and there were no men where there had been four. Our barge headed back toward the destroyer that had carried us to the Admiralties."

By capturing the Admiralties, MacArthur could control the western approaches to the Bismarck Sea, outflank Japanese strongholds on the New Guinea coast, and protect Allied advances into the open waters leading toward the Philippines.

The American invasion began on February 28, 1944, with the landing of 1,000 soldiers on the island of Los Negros in the Admiralties group of the Bismarck Archipelago. The Japanese soldiers confronting MacArthur's invasion force put up a stiff fight. From a U.S. Army report come these excerpts describing the first day's fighting: "There was no sign of enemy opposition until the landing boats reached the line of departure, 3,700 yards from the beach . . . enemy machine-gun fire opened on the boats, which maneuvered radically as they stood in. . . . When the second wave started in, enemy fire was so heavy from the skidway area and north of it, as well as from the northern point of the harbor entrance, that the boats were forced to turn back until

these points had been bombarded again by the Flusser and the Drayton [Navy Destroyers]. . . . Air participation was limited by a heavy overcast and a low ceiling. Of the 40 B-24's scheduled to arrive during the naval bombardment, only 3 appeared before their appointed time to bomb the target area. . . . The planned missions of four groups of B-25's fared little better, only nine appeared and these later than scheduled."

Despite strong Japanese defensive measures, MacArthur's troops managed to establish a beachhead on Los Negros island. The local Japanese commander quickly decided to launch an all-out attack on the American beachhead that same night. He issued the following orders to an infantry battalion defending the Hyane Harbor sector: "Tonight the battalion under Captain Baha will annihilate the enemy who have landed. This is not a delaying action. Be resolute to sacrifice your life for the Emperor and commit suicide in case capture is imminent. We must carry out our mission with the present strength and annihilate the enemy on the spot. I am highly indignant about the enemy's arrogant attitude. Remember to kill or capture all ranking enemy officers for our intelligence purposes. . . . "

As so many time before, American firepower managed to beat back the Japanese nighttime assault. By daylight, the majority of the Japanese attackers had withdrawn back to the cover of the surrounding jungle. However, a few Japanese stragglers had managed to reoccupy their former pillboxes within the American defensive perimeter. A reporter on the scene described the dangers of trying to flush the Japanese soldiers out of their hiding places: "At about 0730 the divisional wire chief, a captain, passed a pillbox and a Jap shot at him, hitting him in the groin and chest. Lying in the mud 6 feet from the tip of the V-shaped dugout, the captain pointed to the pillbox.

"Pfc. Allan M. Holliday of Miami, Florida, and Cpl. James E. Stumfoll of Pittsburg, Kansas, who were coming up the track when the captain was shot, ducked behind the palms and began firing at the pillbox.

"When four Japs ran out the other entrance, they were cut down by a squad on that side. Holliday and Stumfoll crept up, tossed grenades into the opening near them. The Japs threw back two of the grenades but the others exploded inside the hole.

"There was no noise after that inside, so Holliday and Stumfoll and a handful of other cavalrymen circled to the other entrance and started to pull the palm fronds away from the hole.

"A Jap was sitting up inside, drawing a bead with his rifle. About 20 carbines and tommy guns practically sawed him in half. He folded over like a man in prayer.

"The GIs heard more noises inside the pillbox but didn't bother to find out who was causing it; they just blew the roof in with TNT and grenades, and the battle for this particular pillbox was over."

By the end of March 1944, the Japanese defenders of the Admiralties were so short of ammunition and food that they no longer posed any threat to MacArthur's troops. Of the original 4,300 Japanese defenders estimated

This posed shot shows American soldiers in New Guinea manning an air-cooled Browning .30-caliber machine gun. The soldier in the background is armed with a bolt-action M1903A3 Springfield rifle. MacArthur's campaign to seize the northeast coast of New Guinea was completed by September 1944. In a period of nine months, MacArthur's forces had moved some 1,300 miles up New Guinea. Allied casualties were a little more than 20,000, which included 3,600 killed. Japanese losses totaled over 43,000 men, including some 40,000 killed. *Real War Photos*

Pictured crossing a slow-moving river in New Guinea are these U.S. soldiers. MacArthur had employed nine divisions (with approximately 10,000 to 15,000 men apiece) during his Southwest Pacific campaigns. Of these nine divisions, eight were Army and one was Marine Corps. At least the equivalent of an additional Army division was employed by MacArthur in separate regimental combat teams. All the Army divisions and regimental combat teams that participated in the drive up the New Guinea coast later served in the Philippines. *Real War Photos*

to be deployed in the Admiralties before the American invasion, almost 3,280 were confirmed killed with another 75 captured. American losses were 326 killed, 1,189 wounded, and 4 missing.

Supporting Players

One of the most important elements of MacArthur's campaigns in the Southwest Pacific during World War II was the logistical support provided by the U.S. Army's Transportation Corps. The Transportation Corps had been formed in July 1942 and was charged with "the direction, supervision, and coordination of all transportation functions of the War Department, and with the operation of field installation pertaining thereto." The Transportation Corps was a relatively small service and never numbered more then 100,000 men.

In trying to support MacArthur's forces in the Southwest Pacific during World War II, the Transportation Corps faced a number of major problems. The biggest being the enormous distances involved in waging war in the Pacific. San Francisco, the main port of embarkation supplying MacArthur's forces in the Southwest Pacific, is 6,193 nautical miles from Brisbane, Australia, 5,800 from Milne Bay, New Guinea, and 6,299 from the city of Manila in the Philippines. Ships required more time to sail from the

United States to the Southwest Pacific area and return than to any other area of conflict other then the China-Burma-India area or the Persian Gulf region. The long turn-around time, combined with the fact that many of the ships were commandeered into local service, severely taxed the limited shipping then available.

Another major concern for the Transportation Corps was a worldwide shortage of transport ships. This factor was made even worse since the war in Europe was still considered top priority until early May 1945, when the war against Germany ended.

MacArthur's forces in the Pacific were always highly dependent upon ships and small craft to deliver their men and supplies since local transportation facilities in that part of the world either didn't exist or were so poor that they were almost useless. Even when enough vessels could be found to launch a successful invasion of an enemy-held island, the lack of adequate port facilities meant that the supplies needed to support the onshore combat troops couldn't even be unloaded from the supply ships a few thousand yards offshore from the invasion beachhead positions. This problem first manifested itself at Milne Bay, New Guinea, in September and October 1943. Because the Army and Navy sent more ships to the area than could be unloaded quickly, the harbor at Milne Bay filled up with over 140 ships, some of which had to wait for 40 days before being unloaded. Similar difficulties would plague MacArthur forces until the end of the war. Because onshore storage sites were always at a premium, local commanders began to use Navy cargo ships as floating warehouses. This made the shortage of transport ships even worse in the Southwest Pacific. By January 1945, the Joint Chiefs of Staff directed that all theater commanders stop using Navy supply ships as floating warehouses. MacArthur was very upset with this directive and protested strongly (to no avail) that it would interfere with his impending invasion of the Philippine island of Luzon. Transportation Corps officers, on the other hand, felt that there was no excuse for MacArthur's forces to keep idle large numbers of ships that were desperately needed for other jobs.

Summary

In late February 1944, MacArthur's headquarters staff had issued a report that summed up its view of the Pacific campaign: "We have landed in the Admiralty Islands which stand at the northern entrance to the Bismarck Sea almost due south of Guam and 1,300 miles from the Philippines. . . . This marks a final stage in the great swinging move pivoting on New Guinea which has been the basic purpose of the operations initiated on June 29, 1943, when the Southwest Pacific Area and South Pacific Area were united under General MacArthur's command. The axis of advance has thereby been changed from the north to the west. This relieves our supply line of the constant threat of flank attack which has been present since the beginning of the Papuan campaign. This line, previously so precariously exposed, is now firmly secured not only by air coverage, but by our own front to which it is perpendicular. The operation has been a delicate one and its final success lays a strategically firm foundation for the future. Tactically it tightens the blockade of the enemy's remaining bases. Their supply lines are definitely and conclusively severed and only a minimum of blockade running, by submarine or individual surface craft, is now possible. In addition to the troops trapped in the Solomons, some fifty thousand of the enemy, largely in New Britain and at Rabaul, are now enclosed. Their situation has become precarious and their ultimate fate is certain under blockade, bombardment and the increasing pressure of besieging ground forces. The end of the Bismarck Campaign is now clearly in sight with a minimum of loss to ourselves."

Chapter Three

MacArthur Returns To The Philippines

B y the spring of 1944 the first aim of Allied strategy in the Pacific had been achieved and the pattern of operations was set. There would be no frontal attacks against a

MacArthur was a great fan of theatrical props. He knew they attracted the attention of the press as well as the American public. In World War I, MacArthur adopted the crushed, non-regulation officer's cap as part of his normal attire. During World War II, he adopted his well-known and often-photographed corn cob pipe, as seen in this picture. By the spring of 1944, operations in the Pacific were going so well that the Joint Chiefs ordered MacArthur and Nimitz to make plans to invade Mindanao, the southernmost island of the Philippines, sometime in mid-November 1944. *MacArthur Memorial*

strongly entrenched enemy if they could be avoided, no inch-by-inch trek through the jungle or island-by-island advances across an ocean dotted with numerous atolls and island groups. Instead, U.S. forces would advance by "kangaroo leaps," limited only by the range of land-based air cover or the availability of carrier-borne aircraft, seeking always to deceive and surprise the enemy. The Japanese positions thus bypassed would be left to "wither on the vines," isolated and strategically impotent.

MacArthur's thoughts about island-hopping can be found in a September 1943 press release: "My strategic conception for the Pacific Theater, which I outlined after the Papuan Campaign and have since consistently advocated, contemplates massive strikes against only main strategic objectives, utilizing surprise and air-ground striking power supported and assisted by the fleet. This is the very opposite of what is termed 'island hopping' which is the gradual pushing back of the enemy by direct frontal pressure with the consequent heavy casualties which will certainly be involved. Key points must of course be taken, but a wise choice of such will obviate the need for storming the mass of islands now in enemy possession. 'Island hopping' with extravagant losses and slow progress . . . is not my idea of how to end the war as soon and as cheaply as possible. New conditions require for solution and new weapons require for maximum application new and imaginative methods. Wars are never won in the past."

In early 1944, America's military leaders thought that the preinvasion aerial bombardment of Japan could best be undertaken from airfields in eastern China. However, it was later decided that the best way to reach Japan was across the Pacific rather than through Asia, since in the Pacific the Allies could employ the growing strength of the U.S. Navy's Pacific Fleet and its decisive offensive weapon, the carrier-based aircraft.

This plan of operation would begin with the capture of an island in the central or southern Philippines. From there, the Allies could gain control of the South China Sea and neutralize Japanese air strength on the main island of Luzon. To reach the Philippines, the Allies could follow two routes: one through Admiral Nimitz's Central Pacific Area via the Gilbert, Marshall, and Caroline Islands, and Palaus; the other through General Mac-

The planned landing of American forces on the Philippine island of Leyte on October 20, 1944, fulfilled the long-cherished desire of MacArthur to avenge the humiliating defeat he suffered at the hands of the Japanese military in the early days of World War II. Besides restoring MacArthur's pride, the primary military reason for seizing Leyte was to establish air and logistical bases in order to support future operations on the main Philippine island of Luzon. Pictured are American soldiers unloading supplies on one of the Leyte beachheads. *U.S. Navy*

Pictured under a camouflage net is a U.S. Navy Grumman F4F Wildcat Fighter. In mid-September 1944, carrier-based aircraft from Admiral "Bull" Halsey's Third Fleet attacked the Central Philippines. So feeble was Japanese resistance to that attack, Halsey reported to his boss, Admiral Nimitz, that the Philippines were wide open. When this information was passed on to the Joint Chiefs by Nimitz, they ordered MacArthur and Nimitz to cancel plans to invade Mindanao and instead to invade the Philippine island of Leyte by October 20, 1944. *Real War Photos*

The invasion of Leyte involved more men, guns, ships, and aircraft than had been required for any previous operation in the Pacific. For the first time, ground troops from the Central Pacific and Southwest Pacific were to join and fight the Japanese under a common commander, MacArthur. Having left the Philippines under cover of darkness in a puny PT-Boat, MacArthur returned to the Philippines with the greatest armada of naval vessels seen in the Pacific up to that time. Shown here steaming into battle is a combined formation of U.S. Navy carriers and battleships. *Real War Photos*

Arthur's Southwest Pacific Area via the north coast of New Guinea.

The first promised to force a naval showdown with the Japanese Fleet and, once the Marianas were taken, to provide bases from which the Army Air Force's new B-29 bombers could strike the Japanese home islands. The second route, by way of the Southwest Pacific Area, was shorter and offered land bases for air support along the way. Following both paths at the same time would keep Japanese forces divided and offer numerous opportunities for surprise. The Japanese, kept off balance by the twin drives, would never know at what point the next blow would fall. Trying to defend everywhere at once, they would be unable to concentrate their forces anywhere.

MacArthur was strongly against any approach to Japan other then from his area of command. His opinion on the matter can be seen in a 1944 message to Washington: "The attack from the Southwest Pacific Area departs from a base that is closest to the objective and

Despite an early report that there were no Japanese troops on Leyte, in September 1944, MacArthur's intelligence staff estimated that the Japanese forces on Leyte consisted of 21,700 soldiers. It was believed that the Japanese would commit at least two additional infantry divisions to the defense of Leyte within three days of an American landing. Standing guard, a Japanese soldier has attached palm leaves to his uniform to provide additional shade. *Author's collection*

During the invasion of Leyte, MacArthur was Supreme Commander of all ground forces taking part in the operation. In charge of MacArthur's naval forces was Vice Admiral Thomas C. Kinkaid, seen here (right) conferring with MacArthur in his personal plane. Kinkaid was in charge of all amphibious movements and landings on Leyte. Before taking part in the invasion of Leyte, Kinkaid had commanded a wide range of Navy ships during his career, ranging from battleships to carriers. *MacArthur Memorial*

To support and protect the actual landings on Leyte, Kinkaid, who reported directly to MacArthur, was in control of the Seventh Fleet. This formation was composed of 6 older battleships, 4 light and 4 heavy cruisers, 30 destroyers, 10 destroyer escorts, and 16 small escort carriers. Kinkaid also had control over a large number of gunboats and mortar flotillas, mine sweepers, auxiliary vessels, and underwater demolition teams. Pictured are two of the Navy's older generations of battleships which provided important gunfire support for many Pacific landings like Leyte during World War II. *Real War Photos*

advances against the most lightly organized portion of the enemy's defenses, effecting a decisive penetration. It is the only plan that permits all effective combination of land, sea and air power. The advance can be made by a combination of airborne and seaborne operations, always supported by the full power of land-based aviation and assisted by the fleet operating in the open reaches of the Pacific. A penetration of the defensive perimeter along this line results in by-passing heavily defended areas of great extent that will fall, practically of their own weight, to mopping up operations with a minimum of loss."

Despite MacArthur's desires, the Joint Chiefs of Staff decided that the key to Pacific strategy for reaching Japan was by a coordinated and mutually supporting drive along two axes of advances with one commanded by

Nimitz the other by MacArthur. Priority would be given to the one from the east led by Nimitz across the waters of the Central Pacific.

The Joint Chiefs of Staff believed that the Central Pacific route of approach to the Philippines was preferable because it was shorter and more direct. They felt that MacArthur's forces coming up from the southwest route towards the Philippines was longer and would be more costly in terms of money, men, aircraft, time, and ships.

Once the Joint Chiefs of Staff decided that both Nimitz and MacArthur would lead separate advances on Japan, it was also decided that the two converging forces would come together on the strategic Japanese-held islands of Formosa or Luzon.

The decision on which island should be invaded was not an easy one for either the U.S.

Navy or Army. Both islands had their good points and bad points for any potential invasion. Formosa was closer to the main islands of Japan and would, if captured, allow American B-29 bombers to carry much heavier bomb loads than if they had to fly from Luzon. The capture of Formosa would also allow America to have a direct waterborne supply route to China. At this point in time, China was considered a strategically important element in the American plan to invade Japan.

MacArthur felt very strongly that the reoccupation of all the Philippine Islands was a national obligation and political necessity. In MacArthur's view, to bypass any or all the Philippine islands would destroy American honor and prestige throughout the Far East as well as the rest of the world.

Eventually, the decision was made to take Luzon. A combination of military and political factors swayed the U.S. Navy to the idea that the capture of Luzon made more sense than trying to take Formosa. At the same time that MacArthur was given the green light to invade Luzon, Nimitz was told to go ahead with his plans to capture the Japanese-held islands of Iwo Jima and Okinawa.

Even as MacArthur was arguing for the invasion of Luzon before the Joint Chiefs of Staff, he set his forces rapidly forward along the northern coast of New Guinea. Having secured the Admiralties, he made a long leap,

Pictured on the deck of a Navy battleship is Admiral Nimitz on the left, and Admiral Halsey on the right. The major portion of MacArthur's naval support for the Leyte invasion was Admiral "Bull" Halsey's Third Fleet. In what later proved to be a very serious command organization fault, Halsey, as commander of the powerful Third Fleet, was to coordinate his operations with those of MacArthur but he was still responsible to Nimitz, Commander in Chief, Pacific Ocean Area. *Real War Photos*

Halsey's Third Fleet consisted of four task forces which averaged 23 ships each. Each of the four task forces typically had 2 large aircraft carriers, 2 light carriers, 2 new battleships, 3 cruisers, and 14 destroyers. Unlike Kinkaid's older-model battleships, which were commissioned between 1914 through 1921, Halsey's Third Fleet had the support of more modern battleships like the USS *Alabama,* which is pictured here. Commissioned into service in August 1942, the *Alabama* had a top speed of 28 knots, which allowed it to keep up with the Navy's big carriers. *Real War Photos*

The mission assigned to each task force of Halsey's Third Fleet was to secure air supremacy over the Philippines, protect the landings, and apply unremitting pressure on the Japanese. If the opportunity to destroy the major portion of the Japanese fleet should arise, or could be created, that destruction was to be its primary task. These conflicting missions assigned to the Halsey fleet almost led to complete disaster for MacArthur's invasion of Leyte. Pictured on the deck of a Navy cruiser is an observation plane ready for launch. *Real War Photos*

During the early part of the campaign to capture Leyte, the U.S. Navy bore the brunt of furnishing air support for MacArthur's ground forces. Typical of the naval aircraft used to support the invasion of Leyte was the Vought F4U-1 Corsair. First deployed into service in April 1943, the Corsair is considered by many to have been one of the top fighter planes of World War II. The most important mission assigned to naval aircraft by MacArthur was the neutralizing of any Japanese ships or aircraft within range of the Philippines. *Real War Photos*

bypassing Japanese concentrations at Wewak and Hansa Bay, and landed his forces at Hollandia, Dutch New Guinea, in April 1944, two months ahead of his original schedule.

Traveling up the New Guinea Coast

Allied intelligence services could read most of the secret Japanese Army radio code messages by January 1944. Because of this, MacArthur knew that his Japanese counterparts believed that his next target would be the Hansa Bay area of New Guinea. This would be where the Japanese would concentrate most of their military ground forces on New Guinea. MacArthur therefore decided to seize an area of New Guinea where the Japanese were not expecting him. This would be the Hollandia area of New Guinea which was only lightly defended by roughly 3,000 enemy soldiers. To accomplish this goal, MacArthur would launch a massive amphibious force of over 200 ships and 50,000 men on a 1,000-mile journey behind Japanese lines. The assault troops would be commanded by one of MacArthur's top field commanders, General Walter Krueger. Air support for the invasion of the Hollandia area was provided by both Army ground-based aircraft and Navy carrier-based aircraft.

The seizure of the Hollandia area of New Guinea was an important step for MacArthur's advance on Japan since it had a port capable of basing many of the Navy's warships, cargo ships, and troop transports. American aircraft operating from airfields on Hollandia could control the skies over western New Guinea, fly reconnaissance and bombing missions against the Japanese-held islands of the western Carolines, including the Palaus, and could provide

Onboard an American submarine in the Pacific Ocean, a sailor catches up on his reading while perched above one of the sub's torpedoes. Crammed living conditions were the norm for all submarines of World War II. To support the invasion of Leyte, U.S. submarines from both the Southwest Pacific and Central Pacific were tasked with maintaining an offensive reconnaissance over the most probable Japanese route of advance toward the Philippines. *Real War Photos*

During the invasion of Leyte, Navy submarines from the Central Pacific Command patrolled in the Formosa, Luzon, Tokyo Bay, and Sasebo area, while those from MacArthur's Seventh Fleet patrolled in the area of the Makassar Straits, the Celebes Sea, and the Sulu Sea. Submarines from both areas also maintained strong patrols in the Hainan area of Northern Luzon. Pictured is a typical World War II Navy Fleet Submarine. *Real War Photos*

support for subsequent landing operations along the north coast of New Guinea. PT-Boats operating from the Hollandia area bases could cut off Japanese barge traffic in the region. Most important, the Hollandia region would offer MacArthur's forces a base and staging area for the support of future operations in the Southwest Pacific.

The actual assault on Hollandia began at first light on April 22, 1944. There was only scattered Japanese opposition throughout the campaign. By June 6, 1944, the last Japanese resistance was mopped up. American casualties amounted to only 124 men killed, 1,057 wounded, and 28 missing. Japanese losses were put at 3,300 killed, 611 captured, and an unknown number of wounded. The rest of the Japanese troops would flee into the countryside.

The seizure of Hollandia and some of the surrounding areas brought MacArthur's strategic plan for the approach to the Philippines one step closer to being realized. By setting up an airfield along the New Guinea coast he could push his forces farther afield and still provide them the air cover they needed. In May 1944, covered by aircraft based on the fields won in the Hollandia area, MacArthur's forces jumped ahead another 125 miles to Wakda Island located along the New Guinea coast.

Japanese soldiers advance into battle. Both the Japanese Army and Navy saw MacArthur's invasion of Leyte as their last chance to win a decisive victory over the American military drive on Japan. The Japanese Army, with the help of its Navy, poured thousands upon thousands of men into the ground battle for Leyte. The Japanese Army also committed hundreds of planes to attack MacArthur's shipping as well as his airfields on Leyte. *Author's collection*

Wakda Island had a Japanese-built airfield whose capture would prove very useful to MacArthur's operations in New Guinea. Wakda Island itself was only 3,000 yards long and 1,200 yards wide, and had been a coconut plantation before the war. With only a mixed

In a last desperate attempt to change the tide of the war in the Pacific, the Japanese Navy planned to pounce on the American Third and Seventh Fleets in the water around the Philippines and deliver a knockout blow to the American Navy. After destroying the warships of the U.S. Navy, the Japanese Navy then planned on destroying MacArthur's invasion fleet of cargo and troop ships as well as the American beachhead positions on Leyte. Shown in this aerial view is the Kaga, a Japanese aircraft carrier. *Real War Photos*

bag of Japanese defenders, the island was invaded by MacArthur's forces on May 18, 1944, and declared secure the next day. The airfield was made operational by May 21.

Ten days after the capture of Wakda Island, MacArthur's amphibious forces landed on Biak Island, 325 miles northwest of Hollandia. Biak Island had five Japanese-built airfields that MacArthur wanted. Biak Island was occupied by 11,400 Japanese troops, only 4,000 of them being combat troops. To help defend the island from the American assault, the local Japanese commander had a battery of 75-mm mountain guns, four 120-mm naval dual-purpose guns, three or four 3-inch anti-aircraft guns, and a large number of mortars and automatic weapons of all caliber. Unlike the Japanese troops of the Hollandia area or Wakda Island, who melted away in front of MacArthur's men, the Japanese defenders of Biak Island put up a stiff fight, which caught MacArthur and his commanders by surprise. So fierce were the Japanese counterattacks on

To accomplish its mission of destroying the American Third and Seventh Fleets the Japanese Navy amassed a force of 4 carriers, 7 battleships, 19 cruisers, and 33 destroyers. These ships were divided into four groups, each with its own mission. The largest task force was comprised of 4 Japanese battleships, including the world's largest battleship, the Yamato. Accompanying the battleships were 12 cruisers and 15 destroyers. Pictured is a Japanese Navy cruiser. *Real War Photos*

In a series of four major engagements between October 23 and 25, 1944, the U.S. Navy won a resounding victory over the Japanese Navy. American losses consisted of only 1 light carrier, 2 escort carriers, 2 destroyers, and 1 destroyer escort. Japanese losses were 3 battleships, 1 large carrier, 3 light carriers, 6 heavy cruisers, 4 light cruisers, and 9 destroyers. Even as the remaining Japanese ships retreated from the waters around the Philippines, American carrier-based aircraft like this Grumman TBF Avenger torpedo-bomber continued to attack the Japanese ships, inflicting additional losses. *Real War Photos*

The most serious incident during the Leyte Gulf battles occurred on the evening of October 23, 1944. Admiral Halsey was led to believe that a decoy force of ships was the main body of the Japanese fleet. Following his primary orders from his boss, Admiral Nimitz, to seek out and destroy the Japanese fleet whenever the situation arose, Halsey withdrew his Third Fleet from guarding MacArthur's defenseless troop and supply ships and went after what he took to be the main Japanese fleet. The heart of Halsey's Third Fleet were his large aircraft carriers like the vessel pictured here. *Real War Photos*

Typical of the type of infantry support weapons used by American soldiers in the Pacific is this water-cooled .30-caliber Browning machine gun. Krueger's Sixth Army had about 200,000 troops available for the invasion of Leyte. Of these number, 174,000 were made available for the initial invasion of Leyte. All of the assault divisions were reinforced with tank battalions, joint assault signal companies, and many attached service troops. Army divisions employed in the invasion of Leyte included the 1st Cavalry Division and the 7th, 24th, 32d, 77th and 96th Infantry divisions. *U.S. Army*

Biak that American units were forced to retreat from their positions.

From the official U.S. Army history of World War II comes this extract describing a combat engagement between American and Japanese tanks on the island of Biak: "The 2d Battalion, 162d Infantry, with the 1st Platoon, 603d Tank Company, in support, was astride the main coastal road 1,000 yards east of Mokmer. The battalion's left flank was on the beach while its right was against the coastal cliff and less than forty yards inland. Between the beach and the coconut grove, the main coastal road crossed the rise of the cliff at a point about 475 yards west of the 2d Battalion's lines.

"Shortly after 0800 the Japanese tanks, followed by an infantry column, advanced down the incline where the main road crossed the cliff and deployed in echelon left formation in

Unknown to Halsey, the main Japanese fleet was now headed toward the Leyte beachhead. The only American naval forces that stood between the Japanese main force to deter them from destroying MacArthur ships, planes, and supplies was a small force of escort carriers, destroyers, and destroyer escorts under the command of Admiral Kinkaid's Seventh Fleet. Despite the overwhelming strength of the fast-approaching Japanese main force, Kinkaid's ships and planes put up such a spirited defense that the Japanese naval commander believed he was being attacked by a much larger force and decided to withdraw from the battle. Pictured is the type of small escort carrier that fought so bravely during the Battle of Leyte Gulf. *Real War Photos*

the coconut grove. The Japanese vehicles were light tank. . . . They were opposed by two General Sherman M4A1 medium tanks, the heaviest armament on which was the 75-mm gun. Each Japanese tank was stopped by one round of 75-mm armor-piercing ammunition, while the enemy infantry was literally mowed down by the machine guns and mortars of the 2d Battalion, 162d Infantry. Armor-piercing 75-mm shells passed right through the Japanese light tanks, and the Shermans followed with a few rounds of 75-mm high explosive, which tore holes in the Japanese vehicles and blew loose their turrets. During this action several hits scored on the Shermans by the Japanese 37-mm guns caused no damage."

It wasn't until June 8, 1944, that the heavily reinforced American troops on Biak Island managed to overcome Japanese resistance to capture the first enemy airfield. However, the failure of the American soldiers to seize the area surrounding the airfield meant it still couldn't be used by American aircraft. By mid-June the failure to have an operational airfield on Biak was starting to worry MacArthur and his commanders. Any delay in making the airfields on Biak usable for American aircraft would threaten the speed of future operations within the Southwest Pacific Area.

At the same time as MacArthur's forces were fighting on Biak Island at the end of May 1944, Nimitz was preparing to move into the Marianas Islands, the seizure of which the Japanese Navy believed would be an unparalleled calamity which would foreshadow the loss of the war for them. The danger of these movements was immediately apparent to the Japanese high command. They knew that American planes based at Biak would be able to keep under surveillance and to attack the Japanese fleet assembling in Philippine waters. The Japanese decided, therefore, to first drive MacArthur's forces from Biak. Risking major elements of their fleet, the Japanese began sending reinforcements to the island and redeploying to western New Guinea, within reach of Biak, about half the land-based naval aircraft in the Marianas and the Carolinas. In its original plans, the Japanese Navy had counted on these planes for support in the coming battles with the U.S. Navy Pacific Fleet. Unfortunately

The ground troops employed in the invasion of Leyte came from MacArthur's Sixth Army, which was under the able command of General Walter Krueger, seen here conferring with MacArthur. Krueger was an old friend of MacArthur. Born in Prussia, Krueger was not commissioned an officer out of West Point like MacArthur and most other U.S. Army generals. Instead, Krueger rose through the ranks, having first joined the U.S. Army in 1898 as a private. *MacArthur Memorial*

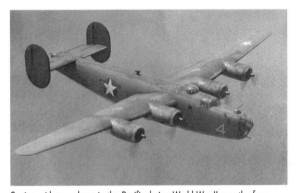

Seeing widespread use in the Pacific during World War II was the four-engined Consolidated B-24 Liberator bomber, as pictured here. For the invasion of Leyte, MacArthur's land-based aircraft of the Far East Air Forces were under the command of Major General George C. Kenney. His job was to use his aircraft to neutralize any Japanese planes or ships within range of the Philippines. On orders from MacArthur, Kenney was also responsible for taking over the mission of furnishing direct air support for the troops on the ground in Leyte. *U.S. Army*

for the Japanese Navy, most of their pilots who made the flight to western New Guinea were immediately stricken with malaria or other tropical diseases on arrival and could play no important role in the upcoming battles.

The Japanese made two partially successful attempts to reinforce Biak. For the third try, they assembled sufficient naval strength to overwhelm local Allied naval units under General MacArthur's overall command. But just as this last naval force began moving toward Biak, the Japanese learned that the U.S. Navy Pacific Fleet was off the Marianas. The Japanese quickly reassembled their fleet and sailed northeast to meet the American Navy. In the engagement that followed, the Battle of the Philippine Sea, the Japanese, who had lost their land-based air support and all chances of surprising the Americans, went down in defeat. Again the carrier task forces of the U.S. Navy Pacific Fleet proved themselves the decisive element of the Pacific war, with their victory over the Japanese fleet paving the way for success in the Marianas and at Biak (which was declared secure on August 20, 1944).

By June 15, 1944, Nimitz's forces were in

Pictured inside the turret of a U.S. Navy cruiser are sailors preparing to load "personalized" 8-inch shells into their ship's main guns. Fire-support from U.S. Navy warships was an important element in almost every island invasion in the Pacific. U.S. naval gunfire was the most feared and most effective of all weapons used against Japanese troops resisting a landing and assault. Without exception, Japanese prisoners of war stated that naval gunfire prevented their movement by day or night and was the most deciding factor in accomplishing their many defeats in the Pacific during World War II. *Real War Photos*

the Marianas, where Marine Corps and Army troops secured Saipan, Guam, and Tinian after a month of bloody fighting. This invasion had drawn the Japanese fleet into battle, and U.S. Navy fast-carrier forces had inflicted on it a crippling defeat. Control of the Marianas now brought the Japanese homeland within reach of the Army Air Force's B-29 bombers, which in late November 194, began to blast and burn the cities of Japan.

Even before the invasion of the island of Biak by MacArthur's forces, his headquarters staff had considered the necessity of occupying other islands in the area to protect the gains which might be achieved with the capture of Biak Island. The capture of another island in the area might also provide an additional air base from which American aircraft could attack the Vogelkop Peninsula, the last Japanese stronghold on Western New Guinea. Finally, on June 4, 1944, MacArthur's staff chose the island of Noemfoor for its plan. It was located about halfway between the island of Biak and the Japanese base at Manokwari on the northeast tip of the Vogelkop Peninsula, and had two Japanese-built airstrips which MacArthur's commanders wanted to use for their own aircraft.

Noemfoor Island was being used by the Japanese as a way station for troops moving to reinforce Biak Island. The island itself had only 2,000 troops on it. Of these, only 900 could be considered combat troops.

The attack on Noemfoor Island began on July 2, 1944. Little organized Japanese resistance was encountered. In conjunction with the naval landing, there was also a large airborne assault on the island by over 1,500 paratroopers of the 503rd Parachute Infantry Regiment on July 3 and July, 4. Casualties from enemy action were nil. But, over 10 percent of the paratroopers that were dropped on the island suffered serious injuries due to landing accidents. Following formations were landed by transport planes directly on the former Japanese airfield.

Combat action on Noemfoor consisted mainly of hunting down small units of Japanese stragglers. During one such patrol, Sgt. Ray E. Eubanks, a squad leader of the 503rd Parachute Infantry took action that earned

Bringing the assault troops of the Sixth Army onto the beaches of Leyte were a vast array of specialized landing craft that had been quickly developed during the early stages of the war and then rushed into production. The largest vessel built especially for landing on enemy beaches was the Landing Ship Tank (LST), as pictured. Many World War II veterans will tell you that LST really stood for "Large Slow Target." Others referred to them as "floating boxcars." *U.S. Navy*

him the Congressional Medal of Honor. Leading his squad to the relief of a platoon isolated by the Japanese, Sgt. Eubanks was wounded and his rifle rendered useless by Japanese fire. He continued to lead his squad forward, using his rifle as a club. By this means he killed four more Japanese before he himself was again hit and killed.

The island of Noemfoor was declared secure on August 31, 1944. Japanese losses were put at 1,730 killed and another 186 captured. American losses were 63 killed, 343 wounded, and 3 missing.

Finding the main Japanese airfield on Noemfoor unsuitable for heavy use, MacArthur ordered that an entirely new airfield be built. This job was completed by September 2, 1944. American aircraft flying from this airfield would go on to support MacArthur's invasions of the Vogelkop Peninsula and Morotai Island.

The capture of the Vogelkop Peninsula was seen by MacArthur as the final large-scale operation his forces would conduct in New Guinea. With the building of new airfields in the Vogelkop Peninsula, his planes could support future operations in the Mindanao area of the Philippines, or if necessary, via the Japanese-held islands located between the Vogelkop

Despite their less-than-perfect design, the large and ungainly LSTs that took part in the numerous campaigns of the Pacific earned the respect of the sailors who manned them. One commanding officer of an LST stated in a wartime report: "An LST is the only ship in the world of 4,000 tons or over that is continuously rammed onto and off coral, sand and mud." LSTs could carry up to 13 medium tanks or 20 light tanks. Pictured here is an M4 Sherman tank coming off an LST. The diesel-powered LSTs had an overall length of almost 328 feet, a width of 50 feet, and a draft of roughly 14 feet when fully loaded. *U.S. Navy*

and Mindanao. With little in the way of real Japanese opposition, MacArthur's forces landed on the Vogelkop Peninsula on July 30, 1944. By August 31, 1944, the ground operations were over except for some minor patrolling.

In mid-September 1944, MacArthur sent his forces out to capture the lightly defended Japanese-held island of Morotai. The island was located between New Guinea and the Philippine island of Mindanao. MacArthur wanted the island as a stepping stone for his future invasion of Mindanao. Once in his control, MacArthur had built both a large naval supply base and a number of airfields on the island from which his ground-based aircraft could protect and support his invasion forces during their assault on Mindanao.

Some Conclusions

At the same time, MacArthur was planning for his long-awaited first step back into

Another specialized Navy landing craft that played an important part in the many island landings of MacArthur's forces in the Pacific was the Landing Craft Infantry (LCI). Nicknamed "lice" by American soldiers and sailors, the vessel weighed about 380 tons and was diesel-powered. Each one was 157 feet long and had a width of 23 feet. It had a top speed of about 12 knots on smooth seas. An LCI could carry 205 troops and 32 tons of cargo in addition to its normal ship's company and normal stores. *U.S. Navy*

the Philippine Islands. Nimitz's Navy and Marine Corps units were engaged in a bloody but successful struggle to secure the eastern approaches to the Luzon-Formosa-China coast region, the strategic target area where the Joint Chiefs of Staff had decided that MacArthur's forces were to meet with Nimitz's forces before advancing on the Japanese homeland.

In a period of a little more than a year, MacArthur's forces had advanced over 1,300 miles and cut off some 135,999 enemy troops. In less time than that, the U.S. Navy and Marine Corps had moved forward from Hawaii to the western Carolinas, a distance of almost 3,000 miles. The stage was therefore set for the retaking of the Philippines.

While many of America's top military and government leaders of World War II had strong doubts about supporting two major campaigns against Japan, the risk that the United States incurred in the Pacific by dispersing its forces and conducting two strategic offensives at the same time brought some rewards. The Japanese could never know for sure from which direction the next American offensive would come. As combat losses depleted Japanese air and naval forces and interdiction of supply lines cut off ground units, the Japanese military lost the initiative with which they started the war; confronted with increasingly strong and aggressive American and Allied forces in both the South and Southwest Pacific, the Japanese would never regain it. American destruction of Japanese troops, their supplies, and their means of transportation throughout the northern Solomons and New Guinea left the Japanese mired in a multi-front war they could not win.

On to the Philippines

When attempting to land on hostile shores, LSTs were normally supported by other, more-heavily-armed naval vessels ranging from destroyers up to battleships. It was the job of these vessels to use their weapons to destroy any enemy defensive positions before the LSTs were sent in to land. This didn't always work as it was supposed to, or course. Navy destroyers were often called upon to screen LSTs by escorting them right up to their landing beaches. Pictured here is a U.S. Navy Fletcher-class destroyer, the USS Lardner. *Real War Photos*

In a March 1943 message to Washington, MacArthur stated his strong belief that by attacking the Philippines, the war in the Pacific could be ended much quicker than by any other path: "In my opinion, purely military considerations demand the reoccupation of the Philippines in order to cut the enemy's communications to the south and to secure a base for our further advance; even if this were not the case and unless military factors demanded another line of action, it would in my opinion be necessary to reoccupy the Philippines. It is American territory, where our unsupported forces were destroyed by the enemy; practically all of the seventeen million Filipinos remain loyal to the United States and are undergoing the greatest privation and suffering because we have not been able to support or succor them; we have a great national obligation to discharge. I feel also that a decision to eliminate the campaign for the relief of the Philippines, even under appreciable military considerations, would cause extremely adverse reactions among the citizens of the United States; the American people, I am sure, would acknowledge the obligation."

The main strategic objective in the Philippines was Luzon. It was believed that the Japanese would mass on Luzon a formidable concentration of ground, air, and naval strength. MacArthur and the Joint Chiefs had originally planned to seize their first foothold in the Philippines on southern Mindanao, as far as possible from enemy air and naval bases in Luzon, and then, proceeding to Leyte in mid-December, establish further bases from which to gain air supremacy over the main objectives. But in September 1944, Admiral Halsey, striking at the central and southern Philippines with his fast carriers in support of the landings on the Palau Islands and Morotal, discovered few signs of enemy ground,

Unlike the larger LSTs, which unloaded troops and cargo through two large front doors, early models of the smaller LCIs discharged troops and equipment by means of gangways hinged to a platform on the front of the vessel. Despite its low draft of roughly 4 feet when fully loaded, troops normally had to wade through shoulder-high water to reach dry land. The LCI was operated by two officers and 22 enlisted men. Due to their smaller size, LCIs were normally armed only with a few 20-mm antiaircraft guns and some .50-caliber machine guns. Here is an interesting overhead shot of an LCI. *U.S. Navy*

naval, or air activity in the islands.

MacArthur and Nimitz, therefore, both proposed going directly to Leyte in October 1944. The Joint Chiefs of Staff, then meeting with the British Chiefs of Staff at Quebec, Canada, quickly issued the necessary orders. The attack on Mindanao and ones planned against Yap Island were canceled, and the Third Amphibious Forces, containing an Army corps of three divisions with which Nimitz was to have taken Yap, was added to MacArthur's forces for the assault on Leyte. The decision to go to Leyte was strategically very wise since it would force the Japanese to split their forces in the Philippines and virtually compel the Japanese Fleet to come out into the open to meet this threat to their inner defensive line.

For the Leyte operation the Central Philippine Attack Force, which included the Seventh

A bit smaller than an LCI was the Landing Craft, Mechanized (LCM) Mark 3, as shown here unloading a truck. Roughly 50 feet long and about 14 feet wide, the diesel-powered LCM was capable of carrying up to 30 tons. This enabled it to carry almost any type of wheeled or tracked vehicle in the American inventory (one at a time). As a troop transport, the LCM could carry up to 60 men. Top speed of the LCM, unloaded, was about 11 knots. Fully loaded, the top speed dropped down to about 8 knots. *Real War Photos*

Larger than the LCM was the Landing Craft Tank (LCT), as pictured here unloading Army ambulances. This diesel-powered vessel had a crew of 13 and could carry either five medium tanks or nine trucks. Almost 1,000 of these vessels were built for the U.S. Navy during World War II, and they saw heavy use in both the Pacific and Atlantic. These vessels were far from perfect. Their low speed of 6 knots limited their daily staging in combat areas to about 100 miles per night. In poor sea conditions, the speed of an LCM could drop to as low as 2 knots. *U.S. Navy*

Fleet, was under the command of Vice Admiral Thomas C. Kinkaid. The Central Philippines Landing Forces, which included all the U.S. Sixth Army troops, was under General Walter Krueger. Land-based air forces were under the control of General George C. Kenney. Mac-Arthur was in supreme command. Halsey's Third Fleet, which remained under Nimitz's command, was to protect the north flank of the invasion force against any attacks by the Japanese Combined Fleet and furnish air support for the neutralization of enemy air power, particularly in the northern and central Philippines. Thus, only part of the naval forces assigned to the operation was under Mac-

Arthur's command. The weaknesses inherent in this departure from unity of command were revealed at a most critical moment in the Leyte invasion.

With four Army divisions landing at different locations, MacArthur's forces went ashore at Leyte Gulf on October 20, 1944, in the largest amphibious assault then mounted in the Pacific.

On the same day his troops landed on the island of Leyte, MacArthur came ashore to give a speech, over a portable radio set, to millions of waiting Filipinos in which he announced: "This is the Voice of Freedom, General MacArthur speaking. People of the

Philippines: I have returned. By the grace of Almighty God our forces stand again on Philippine soil—soil consecrated in the blood of our two peoples. We have come, dedicated and committed to the task of destroying every vestige of enemy control over your daily lives, and of restoring, upon a foundation of indestructible strength, the liberties of your people.

"At my side is your President, Sergio Osmena, worthy successor of that great patriot, Manuel Queron, with members of his cabinet.

The seat of your government is now therefore firmly re-established on Philippine soil.

"The hour of your redemption is here. Your patriots have demonstrated an answering and resolute devotion to the principles of freedom that challenges the best that is written on the pages of human history.

"I now call upon your supreme effort that the enemy may know from the temper of an aroused and outraged people within that he has a force there to contend with no less violent than is the force committed from without.

The best-known amphibian vehicle employed by both the U.S. Army and Navy during the war in the Pacific was the Landing Vehicle, Tracked (LVT), shown here coming ashore. Other names for this vehicle were Amtrac or Alligator. Designed at first as only a non-armored amphibian troop and cargo carrier, the first production LVT (known as the LVT1) was powered by two Hercules 6-cylinder gasoline engines. Later models were outfitted with add-on armor to protect the crew and passengers from enemy fire. Roughly 1,225 were built during World War II before this vehicle was replaced by improved models. *U.S. Navy*

"Rally to me. Let the indomitable spirit of Bataan and Corregidor lead on. As the lines of battle roll forward to bring you within the zone of operations, rise and strike! For future generations of your sons and daughters, strike! In the name of your sacred dead, strike! Let no heart be faint. Let every arm be steeled. The guidance of Divine God points the way. Follow in His name to the Holy Grail of righteous victory."

MacArthur's amphibious troops had gotten ashore without undue difficulty and

To replace the LVT1, American manufacturers started production of the non-armored LVT2 in 1943. Pictured dragging cargo along a beach is a non-armored LVT2, which had a stronger engine and a greater cargo carrying capacity than the LVT1. Nicknamed the "Water Buffalo," almost 3,000 were built during the war years. This vehicle proved to be the chassis upon which other versions were built, the first of which was the armored LVT(A)1, also known as the "Amtank." This vehicle was basically similar to the LVT2 but had an enclosed hull and mounted a turret armed with a 37-mm gun. *U.S.*

against little initial opposition, but their progress inland was not easy. The Japanese, originally intending to make their main stand on the island of Luzon, now decided to concentrate their remaining air and naval forces against the Americans on Leyte. To maintain their local air superiority and strike at Allied shipping in Leyte Gulf, they reinforced their land-based air forces in the Philippines. More important, they dispatched the remainder of their battle fleet toward Leyte Gulf to destroy the American naval forces and cut the Allied line of communications to the Philippines.

The ensuing naval-air battle for Leyte was perhaps one of the most decisive of the Pacific war. During this battle, Halsey made the decision to pull out of the central Philippines with the major part of his fleet in order to intercept

The LVT(A)4 was developed to replace the LVT(A)1. Very similar to the LVT(A)1, it was fitted with the open-topped turret of an M8 self-propelled vehicle with a mounted 75-mm howitzer. This allowed the LVT(A)4 to engage in both direct and indirect fire missions. Pictured at full speed in the water is this LVT(A)4. *U.S. Navy*

Heading into a Pacific jungle in this great shot is an LVT(A)1. The gun-armed turret for the LVT(A)1 came from the M5A1 light-tank series. The power-operated turret mounted both a gyro-stabilized 37-mm high-velocity gun and a single-coaxial .30-caliber machine gun. On the rear deck of the vehicle's hull were two ring-mounted .30-caliber machine guns. The vehicle was powered by a 7-cylinder aircraft-type air-cooled radial gasoline engine that could push the vehicle through the water at 7.5 mph. *U.S. Navy*

Another very valuable piece of equipment used in the Pacific during World War II was the amphibian truck, better known by its nickname, "the Duck." Placed into service in 1942, the Duck could operate on land or in the water. It could carry approximately 25 men and their equipment, or a 5,000-pound payload. *U.S. Navy*

an element of the approaching Japanese fleet that he felt was a more dangerous threat. Halsey had reached this decision without telling MacArthur or Kinkaid, commander of the Seventh Fleet. His departure left the landing area exposed to another Japanese force, which luckily was turned back by the fearless action of a much-weaker American naval force commanded by Kinkaid. If Kinkaid's ships and planes had not been able to turn back the enemy ships, the Japanese might have sailed into Leyte Gulf and destroyed MacArthur's troop and supply ships. This near-disaster spelled out clearly the dangers of divided command and left MacArthur even more upset

Built for U.S. Army requirements was the LVT(A)2. Also nicknamed the "Water Buffalo," this vehicle was very similar to the LVT2. The big difference was that this vehicle was built of 1/4-inch-thick steel armor plate (except the cab, which was protected by 1/2-inch-thick armor plate), unlike the non-armored LVT2. Powered by a Continental air-cooled aircraft-type radial gasoline engine, 450 of these vehicles were built during World War II. An LVT(A)2 is pictured heading toward an enemy shore, while in the background an American battleship fires its 16-inch guns in support. *U.S. Navy*

with the U.S. Navy and its lack of support for his goals in the Pacific war.

The Battle for Leyte

Leyte is a mountainous island approximately 115 miles long and 15 miles wide at its narrowest point, and filled with many jungles and swamps. The mountains comprise a formidable range with peaks of over 4,000 feet, with heavy forests that are densely covered with tangled underbrush. Tropical rain, steep cliffs, crooked trails, and the lack of good roads added to the tactical difficulties.

As MacArthur's troops pushed inland from their landing beaches on Leyte, they found their principal resistance came from well-camouflaged Japanese pillboxes and coconut log bunkers. The Japanese had over a quarter of a million troops in the Philippines. On Leyte, there were between 60,000 to 70,000 Japanese

soldiers. While the Japanese knew the next major American attack would be in the Philippines, they were not sure of the time or the place.

In one of those hard-to-believe facts of World War II, the Japanese forces on Leyte would receive most of their information on the American order of battle from radio broadcasts. From a wartime interview with a captured Japanese general comes this extract: "At the time of the landing, the 35th Army Headquarters did not know the number or name of the American units which had landed . . . but within a day headquarters learned. . . . We found out . . . by tuning in on the San Francisco broadcasts; Japanese troops in the combat area were unable to determine their identity. From the same source, we later obtained information which was of considerable help in planning. In fact, that was the only way we could get information. . . . Information was al-

The American military was not the only country to deploy armored amphibious vehicles during World War II. The Japanese Navy developed and deployed an entire series of amphibious vehicles for use by its Marines. The best-known example was the Type 2 KA-MI Amphibious light tank, an example of which is pictured here. Fitted with large pontoons on both the front and rear of the vehicle, the tank was pushed through the water at 6 mph by two propellers driven by the vehicle's engine. The Type 2 was steered in the water by two rudders operated by the vehicle commander. Once on dry land, the crew could release the large pontoons and enter into battle. *Aberdeen Proving Ground Museum*

The initial American landings on Leyte went very well. The local Japanese commander had withdrawn the bulk of his forces from the landing areas out of fear of losing them to the American naval bombardment. General Krueger's Sixth Army only had to deal with a few rearguard Japanese defenders during the first 10 days ashore. Pictured here are American soldiers trying to flush Japanese soldiers from a camouflaged concrete pillbox. *U.S. Army*

ways received through the San Francisco broadcast before reports from our front line units reached headquarters. . . . Since the information came much sooner from the American broadcast than from the Japanese communications, the Army Headquarters depended on the American broadcasts for much intelligence."

Armor on Leyte

Leyte was difficult country, for armored vehicles and tanks often were used in twos and threes in close cooperation with infantry. The swamps and jungle underbrush limited their employment almost entirely to roads. Roadblocks, obstacles, and dug-in positions and pillboxes concealed by high cogan grass, mines, antitank fire, and fanatical Japanese with satchel charges all took their toll. Tanks sometimes pushed on ahead of infantry and were destroyed and sometimes lagged behind and were valueless to the infantry.

In a wartime report prepared by the staff of the Sixth Army comes these extracts: "The tanks and tank destroyers could have been used more frequently and with greater versa-

tility. The tanks and tank destroyers were ideal weapons for the destruction of machine guns, mortars, and other heavy infantry weapons, but the infantry commanders seemed to be unaware of their capabilities. Many commanders employed their armored vehicles down the middle of the road when they could have used them more effectively on the flanks and for envelopments."

General Krueger, commander of the Sixth Army, felt that "the tank destroyer commanders lacked aggressiveness and a skilled director. It was common, however, for armor to be ordered left in rear areas and then suddenly called for in a given situation without opportunity for advance briefing or reconnaissance. Sometimes tanks were used purely as artillery even though other units could have used them properly. In other cases, tanks were called upon to be used when the area was definitely not suitable for heavy tracked vehicles. In some cases where tanks could have been used with great effect they were not used. Infantry commanders felt that tanks were not aggressive and tank commanders felt that infantry failed to understand or support them. Perhaps the only well-reconnoitered and detailed plan for infantry-tank cooperation took place on Breakneck Ridge, leading to the final penetration of the Japanese lines."

The Advance Bogs Down

Miserable weather had bogged down supply vehicles and curtailed air support. The Sixth Army found itself engaged in a struggle through difficult terrain against stubborn resistance. The Army Air Force was unable to build up enough strength on Leyte to stop the Japanese from sending in reinforcements to the island until early in December 1943.

Krueger, the Sixth Army commander, decided to speed up the takeover of Leyte with an amphibious landing on the eastern side of the island near the small coastal city of Ormoc. This landing would be done in conjunction with a strong push overland by his troops into the Ormoc Valley. In this operation, Krueger hoped to secure control of both the valley and the port of Ormoc and thus force the Japanese defenders into the mountains near the western coast of Leyte, where they

On the afternoon of October 20, 1944, after the first few waves of American troops had pushed inland on Leyte, MacArthur decided to leave the U.S. Navy cruiser Nashville and travel ashore by landing craft. Accompanying MacArthur onshore were a number of Philippine officials, media representatives, and members of his staff. In this famous and well-known picture, MacArthur wades ashore with the new Philippine President Sergio Osmena at his side. *MacArthur Memorial*

Shortly after landing on a beachhead at Leyte, MacArthur was given a microphone attached to a portable radio transmitter. MacArthur announced to the people of the Philippines that he had returned as promised. In his short speech addressed to the Filipino people, MacArthur called upon them to rise up against their Japanese oppressors. On the left-hand side of the picture, the gentleman without the helmet is CBS reporter William J. Dunn. On the far right-hand side of the picture, standing slightly behind MacArthur, is the Philippine President Sergio Osmena. *MacArthur Memorial*

MacArthur and staff are shown on one of their numerous Jeep tours around Leyte. For Major General George Kenney, head of MacArthur's land-based aircraft, the capture of two Japanese airfields by Sixth Army troops on Leyte proved to be a big disappointment. Both airfields were too small and unsuitable for use during the island's rainy season. Kenney was very concerned about this since he was soon called upon to take over the job of air support on Leyte from the Navy's carrier-based aircraft. *MacArthur Memorial*

could neither escape nor be reinforced.

On the night of December 6, 1944, the same night that an American naval convoy with the 77th Infantry Division onboard sailed to its landing site at Ormoc Bay, a Japanese convoy of six transports and seven escort ships with reinforcements for Leyte was headed to almost the same place as the American troops were supposed to land. Luckily, American planes spotted the enemy convoy and in the most intense aerial battle of the entire Leyte campaign, sank four of the enemy ships on the morning of the seventh. It was estimated that almost 4,000 Japanese soldiers and sailors lost their lives during this engagement.

On that same morning, the American 77th Division was landed on the shores of Ormoc Bay. While Japanese ground defenses offered little resistance to the American landing, the Japanese launched a fierce aerial offensive against the American ships sitting offshore. In a space of about nine hours the Japanese flew 16 missions against the American ships. While American planes did an excellent job in protecting the convoy, enough enemy planes got through to badly damage five vessels, two of which had to be abandoned and then sunk by American naval gunfire.

On December 10th, the Americans began their attack on the town of Ormoc. Ormoc was the largest and most important commercial center in western Leyte. The Japanese had dug

On October 23, 1944, in the Leyte city of Tacloban, MacArthur announced in a very impressive ceremony the re-establishment of the civilian government in the Philippines, and he named Sergio Osmena as the country's new president. MacArthur's good friend Manuel Quezon, the first president of the Philippines, had died on August 1, 1944. MacArthur is shown reading from his prepared text on the steps of Tacloban's city hall. *MacArthur Memorial*

Two M8 Self-Propelled Howitzers are firing in support of the Sixth Army on Leyte. As the naval battle of Leyte Gulf raged in the waters around the island, the Japanese began a series of massive aerial attacks on MacArthur's supply and troop ships in Leyte Gulf as well as American airfields on the island of Leyte itself. The Japanese were determined to make the battle for Leyte not only a decisive naval conflict, but also a decisive ground and air battle. *Real War Photos*

strong defensive positions around the town. One soldier later wrote that as the American soldiers broke through the Japanese defenses, Ormoc "was a blazing inferno of bursting white phosphorus shells, burning houses, and exploding ammunition dumps, and over it all hung a pall of heavy smoke from burning dumps mixed with the gray dust of destroyed concrete buildings, blasted by . . . artillery, mortar, and rocket fire."

At the same time that MacArthur's men were taking Ormoc, other units were pushing into the Ormoc Valley. The capture of Ormoc and the surrounding area had an important effect on Japanese military strength on Leyte since it cut off a port which had been used to bring in both reinforcements and supplies to the battle on the island.

In one last desperate gamble to take the initiative away from MacArthur's forces on Leyte, the Japanese launched a number of airborne attacks on American airfields in early December 1944. While Japanese paratroopers managed to land on some of the airfields, they did only a small amount of damage to a few planes and some fuel and supply dumps before being killed or captured.

Knowing that the Japanese forces on Leyte were finished, the Japanese commander of Luzon sent a message to the Japanese officer in charge of the defense of Leyte. That message included a warning that "the enemy, who has increased his materiel power and war potential, now threatens, solely on the strength of his materiel superiority, to bear down on Luzon Island despite the heroic and desperate efforts of our sea and air forces as well as the Thirty-fifth Army. In view of the sudden change in

Sixth Army soldiers and an M4 Sherman tank carefully approach a suspected Japanese position on Leyte. By November 5, 1944, American soldiers were approaching the Leyte coastal town of Ormoc, the principal Japanese Army installation on the island. It was from the Ormoc Bay area that the Japanese had been reinforcing the defense of Leyte with additional troops and supplies. *Real War Photos*

the situation, we shall seek and destroy our enemy on Luzon Island, thereby doing our part in the heroic struggle of the Army and avenging many a valiant warrior who fell before the enemy. . . . Be ready to meet your death calmly for our beloved country."

The Japanese High Command had invested heavily in trying to hold on to Leyte. In total, the battle for Leyte would cost the Japanese Army four divisions and several separate combat units. The Japanese Navy would lose 26 major warships, and 46 large transports and merchantmen. The battle for Leyte would also reduce Japanese land-based air capability in the Philippines by over 50 percent.

Lessons Learned

In an after-the-battle critique, General Krueger, the American commander of the Sixth Army, which captured Leyte Island from the Japanese, prepared a report based on his observations gathered during the fighting. His purpose was to honestly evaluate the strong points and weaknesses of the American military tactics used in defeating the Japanese forces on Leyte. Extracts from that report include the following: "Although the primary job of the infantry is to close with the enemy and destroy or capture him, the natural reluctance of American infantryman to engage the enemy had to be overcome. . . . On several occasions, strong combat patrols of platoon [40 men] or company [200 men] strength were sent to feel out enemy positions, but as soon as they made contact with the Japanese the patrols withdrew. They accomplished nothing except to determine the presence of an unknown number of enemy soldiers.

"If more than minor resistance was encountered, the troops frequently fell back and called for fire from supporting weapons. . . . The American soldier was too roadbound. Sometimes resistance along the road stopped the entire division. This opposition could have been eliminated quickly by the employment of simple envelopments and flanking attacks.

"The standard employment of artillery in close support of the infantry again proved to be very effective and was used extensively. However, since the artillery fire enabled the infantry to secure many heavily fortified posi-

tions with few casualties, the infantrymen tended to become too dependent upon the artillery men and expected them to do the work of the infantry."

Many high-ranking American officers, commanding troops fighting in Western Europe, were making the same observations about American soldiers fighting the German Army. In general, the officers and enlisted men of the German Army always considered the artillery branch of the U.S. Army the biggest threat to their military formations. A captured Japanese officer on Leyte told his American captors, in his best estimate, that the losses sustained by his division (10,000 men) were caused by 60 percent artillery fire, 25 percent by mortars, 14 percent by infantry weapons (rifles and machine guns) and 1 percent by aircraft.

In contrast to the very effective use of artillery on Leyte by the U.S. Army, Japanese artillery employment on Leyte was described by an American officer in a wartime report as "remarkably undeveloped" and inefficient, as the guns were used mostly alone or in pairs. The Japanese were unable to mass their artillery fire on any single target. While their artillery positions tended to be very well constructed, the Japanese artillery men placed such a high value on concealment that their guns sometimes had a very limited field of fire.

Despite being seriously under-gunned compared to their American counterparts, the Japanese fought bravely as always and their tactics were much improved over earlier campaigns fought in the Pacific. A wartime report from the U.S. Army's 21st Infantry Division stated that "there were few instances of reckless charges, needless sacrifices or failure to observe known tactical principles."

The fighting on Leyte showed the American soldiers that the most effective weapon for destroying Japanese pillboxes was the 75-mm howitzer mounted on a halftrack. The 105-mm howitzer mounted on a medium tank

Right
On December 15, 1944, MacArthur was made a five star general. This picture shows him with his new star cluster. Because of stiff Japanese resistance on Leyte, MacArthur's promise to the Joint Chiefs that he would be ready to invade the main Philippine island of Luzon on December 20, 1944, was not to happen. *MacArthur Memorial*

chassis proved to be more useful because it was so extremely mobile in a variety of terrains ranging from swamps to mountains. Its off-road ability was so great that it could travel up to seven miles farther than any other vehicle in the American inventory, up the mountain trails of Leyte.

Even before the battle for Leyte was officially over, MacArthur sent a message to Washington in October 1944, in which he described his action on Leyte and its strategic importance for the war in the Pacific: "In a major amphibious operation we have seized the eastern coast of Leyte Island in the Philippines, 600 miles north of Morotai and 2,500 miles from Milne Bay from whence our offensive started nearly 16 months ago. This point of entry in the Visayas is midway between Luzon and Mindanao and at one stroke splits in two the Japanese forces in the Philippines. The enemy's anticipation of attack in Mindanao caused him to be caught unawares in

Leyte and beachheads in the Tacloban area were secured with small casualties. The landing was preceded by heavy naval and air bombardments which were devastating in effect. Our ground troops are rapidly extending their positions and supplies and heavy equipment are already flowing ashore in great volume. The troops comprise elements of the 6th U.S. Army, to which are attached units from the Central Pacific, with supporting elements. . . . The strategic result of capturing the Philippines will be decisive. The enemy's so-called Greater East Asia Co-Prosperity Sphere will be cut in two. His conquered empire to the south comprising the Dutch East Indies, and the British possessions of Borneo, Malaya and Burma will be severed from Japan proper. The great flow of transportation and supply upon which Japan's vital war industry depends will be cut as will the counter supply of his forces to the south. A half million men will be cut off without hope of support and with ultimate

The crew of an M8 armored car prepare to fire on a Japanese position on Leyte. The M8 armored car had a four-man crew and was armed with a 37-mm high-velocity gun and at least one onboard machine gun. By December 1, 1944, there were seven Army divisions ashore on Leyte and five airfields in operation. On December 10, the Japanese stronghold of Ormoc was captured, together with large quantities of enemy supplies and equipment. Some Japanese survivors fled to the hills of Leyte. *Patton Museum*

Taking cover from heavy Japanese machine-gun fire, these American soldiers crouch low in a large bomb crater. To speed up his planned invasion of Luzon, MacArthur decided not to wait for the Japanese soldiers on Leyte to give up the fight. Instead, he simply announced to the world on December 25, 1944, that the campaign on Leyte was over. For the American soldiers who fought and died on Leyte during the next four months, until the last Japanese defenders were either killed or captured, MacArthur's announcement of December 25 was a sad joke. *U.S. Army*

destruction at the leisure of the Allies a certainty. In broad strategic conception the defensive line of the Japanese which extends along the coast of Asia from the Japan Islands through Formosa, the Philippines, the East Indies, to Singapore and Burma will be pierced in the center permitting an envelopment to the south and to the north. Either flank will be vulnerable and can be rolled up at will."

After Leyte was taken, the choice of targets lay between Luzon and Formosa, and for many months the Joint Chiefs debated the matter. In the meantime the build-up in the Pacific and subsidiary operations continued. The Japanese, having overrun the airbase sites in eastern China, and the Marianas having provided the B-29 bases needed for bombing Japan, the Joint Chiefs decided in favor of Luzon. MacArthur decreed that he would go there from Leyte in late December 1944, three months before Nimitz could have invaded Formosa.

Chapter Four

The Battle For Luzon

In January 1945, MacArthur had the sweet satisfaction of returning to the main Philippine island of Luzon with a massive American invasion force behind him. In a complete reversal of roles, the Japanese commander on Luzon now found himself in the same position that MacArthur had found himself three years earlier when confronting a Japanese invasion force which had control of both the seas around the Philippines and complete air superiority.

Unlike MacArthur, the Japanese general in command of the forces on Luzon decided that it was foolish trying to defeat the invading American forces on the beaches. Like MacArthur's American and Philippine forces in early 1942, the Japanese forces on Luzon (roughly 270,000 men) were at that time underfed, under-powered, and under-equipped. With little hope of reinforcements or additional supplies, the Japanese commander decided to deploy his troops in the mountainous areas of Luzon, which would provide his forces with natural defensive positions.

In commenting on the Japanese tactics of withdrawing to inland defensive positions instead of meeting invading American forces on the beaches of Luzon, a Japanese officer commented in a postwar interview: "It was indicated from the Battle of Leyte that such tactics would have resulted in a great loss of troops to us. Rather than take such a risk and lose so much, it seemed wiser to remain in the hills and take a delayed action strategy."

In contrast to MacArthur's 1942 decision to retreat to the Bataan Peninsula when pressed by the Japanese, the Japanese commander of the forces on Luzon in January 1945 decided that Bataan would be a death-trap for his troops. Confined to a limited area with little or no real food supply, the Japanese commander rightly believed that superior American firepower would cut his troops to pieces in a very short time.

For MacArthur and his troops the first step in the invasion of Luzon was the seizure of the southwest corner of Mindoro Island, 150 miles south of Manila, on December 15, 1944. The object of this move was to gain air

At 7:00 A.M. on the morning of January 9, 1945, the fire support vessels of MacArthur's invasion fleet opened up on the Lingayen landing beaches of western Luzon. This picture, taken from the tail end of the U.S. Navy cruiser *Minneapolis,* shows the vessel's main guns firing at Japanese shore batteries on Luzon. One of the cruiser's many twin 40-mm antiaircraft guns are visible in the foreground. *Real War Photos*

Posing for this wartime picture, Marines man the 20-mm antiaircraft guns of a Navy battleship. Under command of Admiral Kinkaid's Seventh Fleet, the pre-invasion and covering force for MacArthur's invasion of Luzon consisted of 164 ships. The major striking power of this force were 6 battleships, 6 cruisers, 12 escort carriers, and over 39 destroyers and destroyer escorts. On the trip to the Lingayen Gulf, these ships had to endure murderous kamikaze attacks. These aerial attacks continued once the ships reached their bombardment positions off the Luzon coast. *Real War Photos*

bases from which to support operations on Luzon. After making feints at southern Luzon to mislead the Japanese as to their real point of attack, MacArthur's forces invaded Luzon itself on January 9, 1945, landing along the shores of Lingayen Gulf. This was the same place that the main Japanese landing took place on Luzon in late December 1941.

American efforts to mislead the Japanese forces about their invasion plans were not really needed at that point in time. Having suf-fered such grievous losses in men, planes, and ships during the fight for Leyte, the ability of the Japanese high command or the local commanders to see what MacArthur forces were doing had disappeared. The Japanese were, in effect, blind, and they could no longer plan for any future engagements. Instead, they could only react to American offensive actions after they had occurred.

From a postwar interrogation of Japanese officers involved in the defense of the Philip-

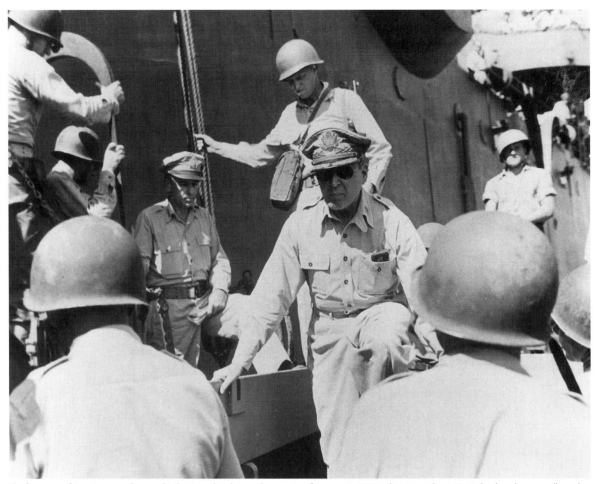

The first wave of American assault troops hit the Luzon beaches on the morning of January 9, 1945. This picture shows MacArthur boarding a small naval landing craft on the first day of the invasion for his trip to the landing beaches. By the end of the first day, the Luzon beachhead was 17 miles long and 4 miles deep. Large numbers of men and great quantities of supplies were safely ashore. *MacArthur Memorial*

pines came this statement by a general officer: "American intelligence was so far superior that a comparison is useless. It seemed to me if we were fighting our battles blindfolded, while the enemy seemed to have ten times the intelligence we had."

The Joint Chiefs of Staff announced the landing on Luzon to the America public and the world at large in a communiqué dated January 10, 1945: "Our forces have landed in Luzon. In a far-flung amphibious penetration our troops have seized four beachheads in Lingayen Gulf. . . . The decisive battle for the liberation of the Philippines and the control of the Southwest Pacific is at hand. General MacArthur is in personal command at the front and landed with his assault troops. His ground forces of the Sixth Army are under General Krueger, his naval forces of the Seventh Fleet

and Australian Squadron are under Admiral Kinkaid, and his air forces of the Far East Air Force are under General Kenney. The Third Fleet under Admiral Halsey is acting in coordinated support."

Tank Battles

As MacArthur's ground forces advanced into the heart of Luzon's central plains, the Japanese commander of Luzon made an effort to defend Highway 5—one of the few key highways that ran across the island. To accomplish this task, he decided to deploy the only Japanese armored division in the Philippines around the Munoz-Lupao-San José area of Luzon.

Despite the overwhelming superiority in firepower enjoyed by MacArthur's troops in retaking Luzon, the tenacity of the Japanese fighting man throughout the war in the Pacific made any offensive operation by American soldiers potentially very costly in lives lost. An example of this can be seen even in the attempted recapture of a small Philippine town like Munoz.

The town itself was an excellent defensive position for the Japanese armored unit. The town was on flat terrain except for a railroad track which leveled off about 100 yards from a large rice mill and a drainage ditch which was in a deep ravine on the west end of the town. The many trees lined with undergrowth located on the north and west end of the town gave its Japanese defenders great cover while the approaches to the town offered little cover for any American attackers. The town had been hit by the American preinvasion aerial bombardment like so many other Philippine towns.

This picture shows MacArthur aboard a borrowed jeep on the main Luzon landing beach. Once the bulk of his ground forces were on Luzon, MacArthur's grand plan was to send a large portion of his forces down the Central Plain of Luzon to recapture his beloved city of Manila. He was convinced that the Japanese would not defend Manila, and he was also positive that he could retake all of Luzon within six weeks' time. Much like the capture of Leyte, which took far longer then he planned, the liberation of most of Luzon would take more than six months and cost almost 47,000 American dead and wounded. *MacArthur Memorial*

The initial Luzon landings were virtually unopposed and assault troops advanced rapidly inland until they came to rugged terrain and well-prepared Japanese defensive positions. Yet the Japanese defenders had skillfully utilized the advantages of the Philippine terrain to protect the strategic passes and roadways of Luzon with heavily fortified and mutually supporting cave and tunnel systems, fully supplied with all types of automatic weapons, mortars, and artillery. Pictured are American soldiers using flame throwers to burn out a Japanese bunker. *Real War Photos*

However, the town had two large concrete rice mill buildings which had withstood the bombing, and there was also a stone schoolhouse. The rest of the town, which had consisted of tin-roofed earthen huts, had been leveled.

On January 30, 1945, the leading elements of an American infantry division approached Munoz when it was fired on by Japanese machine guns. Pinned down, they were only able to withdraw when supporting mortar units laid down a smoke screen. During the rest of that day, American soldiers tried to approach the town from various directions but were stopped by heavy machine-gun fire. That same afternoon, a U.S. Army artillery liaison plane reported seeing tank tracks throughout the town but no Japanese tanks themselves.

Harassing fire was therefore placed on the town, and a night patrol attempted to infiltrate but without success. The Japanese continued to fire flares and opened fire with their machine guns at every opportunity. However, they did not disclose the existence of any heavier weapons to the attacking American

Aided by Filipino civilians, American soldiers are blasting a Japanese pillbox on Leyte with TNT. MacArthur's troops on Luzon found that Japanese soldiers had burrowed so deep into the steep slopes of the Philippine hills and mountains that artillery and mortar fire would not always dislodge them from their positions. The only sure proof way of destroying these Japanese positions was by using American aircraft to dive-bomb the openings of the enemy caves. *U.S. Army*

The soldiers of MacArthur's Sixth Army found that the 2.36 rocket launcher (bazooka) could be used most efficiently in coordination with mortars, machine guns, and rifle fire. The short ranges of the bazooka invariably meant that the bazooka teams would draw heavy return fire unless its fire was coordinated with the fire of other weapons to muffle the distinctive sound and flash of the bazooka. Pictured is a bazooka team from the 1st Cavalry Division ready to fire. Notice that the bazooka gunner has his eyes closed and his loader has his finger in his ear. Behind them, a Signal Corps photographer composes the shot. *Real War Photos*

By January 17, 1945, Sixth Army engineers had finished their first airfield on Luzon, near the landing beaches. Once this airfield was completed, Major General George Kenney's Far Eastern Air Forces assumed responsibility for the air support of all ground operations. By this time there were no more than 10 Japanese planes left on Luzon. What few planes the Japanese had not lost on the ground or in the air had been evacuated to the island of Formosa. Pictured on a grass field is a shark-painted Lockheed P38 Lightning. *Real War Photos*

soldiers. For the American officer in charge, it quickly became obvious that taking the town of Munoz was going to be more than a company-sized operation. Additional troops were therefore ordered in to prepare for another attempt to capture the town.

On the morning of January 31, 1945, a battery of American 105-mm howitzers laid a brief concentration on the town and American infantrymen started to approach the town but again were pinned down. Artillery and mortar fire were laid on the area and the American GIs withdrew under cover of smoke. Preparations were made to use other units during the next attack on the following day.

At 7:45 A.M. on February 1, 1945, American soldiers attacked the large concrete rice mill following a 15-minute artillery preparation by a battalion of artillery. Now the Japan-

ese defenders of Munoz began to disclose more of their defense positions by fire from their 105-mm howitzers and high-velocity 47-mm fire from their dug-in tanks. After a smoke screen was laid, the advancing American infantrymen managed to clear the rice mill but again were halted by heavy Japanese defensive fire. The American soldiers spotted two dug-in Japanese tanks along with a field gun, and these weapons were destroyed by artillery and mortar fire.

The American officer in charge of the assault on Munoz then ordered another infantry battalion to attack from the south of the town but it, too, was stopped by heavy defensive fire. This attack remained stalled until a very brave company commander crawled within point-blank range of a dug-in Japanese tank and succeeded in hitting it with a rifle grenade.

On February 2, 1945, a company of American tanks supported by two battalions of self-propelled guns swung around the town of Munoz to cut off any escape attempt by its Japanese defenders. That morning two American infantry battalions launched another attack on the town following a 15-minute artillery barrage by more than five battalions of artillery, but again the infantry attack was pinned down. During the attack the Americans did manage to set one Japanese tank on fire while two others were destroyed in position by white phosphorus shells fired by heavy mortars. At noon of that same day, three Japanese tanks which attempted to back out of their defensive positions were destroyed by antitank fire, and two more were set on fire in the afternoon. The American commander then ordered another advance on the town. This assault, like the others, was unsuccessful and also very costly in American lives. Americans' attempts to recover their wounded buddies resulted in even more casualties than had occurred in the attack itself.

The U.S. Army's high-velocity 37-mm antitank gun, as shown here, was considered obsolete by American soldiers fighting in Europe. Yet in the Pacific, it proved to be more suitable for combat than many larger weapons because of its light weight and its size. It weighed 990 pounds, compared to its next-larger cousin, the 57-mm antitank gun, which weighed roughly 2,500 pounds. *Real War Photos*

The Japanese replaced the destroyed tanks under cover of darkness, making their position as strong as before but by now their dispositions were more clear. During the night, additional American troops moved into position and on the morning of February 3, another 30-minute artillery preparation at 7:30 A.M. by five artillery battalions and a company of 4.2-inch mortars was followed at 8:00 A.M. by an infantry attack from the south and from the west. At dusk, however, the infantry was still 100 yards from the town and under heavy fire. The Army unit did manage, however, to penetrate a segment of the Japanese first line of defense, destroying a number of tanks and several field

guns but discovered that the Japanese had a second and possibly stronger line behind it.

On the next day, the American infantry soldiers, after repeated assaults, managed to reach the westernmost street in Munoz. By that evening the flanking movement of another American infantry unit managed to set up a roadblock on Highway 5 northeast of Munoz. American artillery and mortar concentrations pounded the Japanese in the town most of the night. Several small banzai attacks were made by the Japanese but all the participants were killed.

The American assault on Munoz continued on February 5th. The infantry continued the

MacArthur's campaign to liberate Luzon involved the largest tank operation in the Pacific by either the Japanese or U.S. military. It marked the first time that the Japanese Army employed one of its few armored divisions against the American military in combat. MacArthur's Sixth Army fielded almost 500 tanks on Luzon between January 1945 and September 1945. The American tank most commonly employed on Luzon was the 32-ton M4 Sherman tank armed with a 75-mm gun. Shown in the Luzon countryside are American infantrymen escorting a Sherman tank. *Real War Photos*

Another American armored vehicle employed in the liberation of Luzon, was the M10 Tank Destroyer, pictured here near the Lingayen Gulf landing beaches. The M10 had a crew of five, and was armed with a 3-inch gun located in an open-topped turret as well as one .30-caliber light machine gun. Based on the modified chassis of the M4 Sherman tank, the vehicle had a top speed of 30 mph. *Real War Photos*

Also employed in the battle of Luzon by MacArthur's Sixth Army was the M5A1 light tank, as shown here on display. The M5A1 light tank had been standardized into American military service in September 1942. The vehicle had a four-man crew, and was equipped with dual driving controls. Armed with a 37-mm high-velocity gun and up to three machine guns, the tank was powered by two water-cooled gasoline engines. The tank's twin engines gave the vehicle a top speed of almost 40 mph. *Patton Museum*

The Japanese commander of Luzon had the 2nd Armored Division at his disposal. This unit was one of only three armored divisions in the entire Japanese Army. Formed in June 1942, the division arrived in the Philippines in September 1944. While missing one of its four regiments, the division could still field about 220 tanks. Most of the tanks in the division were the latest Japanese models. The most numerous model was the Type 97 Medium Tank (Special), such as the one pictured here being examined by curious American soldiers. *Aberdeen Proving Ground Museum*

This is the burned and blackened hulk of a Japanese Type 97 Medium Tank (Special) destroyed in battle. This vehicle was armed with a 47-mm high-velocity antitank gun and a single hull-mounted machine gun. The vehicle had a crew of five and was powered by a Mitsubishi air-cooled diesel engine, which gave it a top speed of 25 mph. A sliding-gear transmission with both a high and low range gave the driver the choice of four forward speeds and one reverse. Armor protection at the thickest averaged no more than 1/4 inch. *Aberdeen Proving Ground Museum*

attack to the northeast, the east, and the north of the town. A counterattack by four Japanese tanks and a platoon of infantry was driven back with high casualties. These same four Japanese tanks then turned south along the town's main street. The leading Japanese tank hit a mine laid in the street the night before and lost a track. An American antitank gun then destroyed the stranded tank at a range of 10 yards and the other three Japanese tanks turned around and fled. An American self-propelled gun moved up to fire on the fleeing Japanese tanks but was hit and set on fire by an unseen Japanese 47-mm antitank gun. Unfortunately, the vehicle's exploding onboard ammunition caused the surrounding American infantry to take cover and then retreat.

There was continued activity on February 6th, including another attack following a 30-minute artillery preparation but the Japanese continued to hold stubbornly. They still held two-thirds of Munoz; 36 of their tanks had been destroyed but they had 20 left plus four artillery pieces.

During the night of February 6, the American commander decided to withdraw his forces to the south of the town and to order a napalm air strike on the town the next day. What he didn't know was that the Japanese commander in Munoz had already decided that same night to retreat from Munoz on the morning of January 7. The Japanese were not aware that their escape route had already been cut by the American troops.

A Japanese diversion attack began at 3:00 A.M. on February 7, and caused considerable confusion among the surrounding American troops. However, the leading Japanese tank was hit by a bazooka round and after the others spread out, a second one was hit by a 37-mm antitank gun. Two of the tanks reached the main highway and sped northeast. The infantry accompanying them had already been killed. Artillery fire was quickly called down on the town, knocking out six more Japanese tanks, several trucks, and a captured American M3 halftrack and towed 105-mm howitzer that the Japanese had been using.

The main enemy column, headed by tanks and truck-mounted infantry, dashed out of Munoz with its headlights on. A U.S. Army roadblock and heavy artillery fire stopped a few vehicles, but two American artillery pieces were overrun. The rest of the Japanese column continued to flee Munoz until it ran head-on into an American tank battalion, which completely destroyed what was left of the column.

In this seven-day action, 56 Japanese armored vehicles were destroyed and almost 2,000 Japanese soldiers were killed. American losses were 97 killed and 303 wounded.

One of the few surviving staff officers of the Japanese 2nd Armored Division that fought on Luzon was quoted thusly in a postwar interview conducted by the American Army: "The employment of the tank division in the Philippines is generally considered a great blunder. The fact remains that the American forces had command of the air, prevented movement along the highways and cross-country movement in an area covered with rice paddies was impossible. Consequently, even though the tanks were organized for

The Japanese 2nd Armored Division on Luzon was equipped with a small number of self-propelled guns mounted on Type 97 medium tank hulls. This picture shows a captured Type 38 Ho-Ro 150-mm self-propelled howitzer. Entering Japanese service in 1942, only a small number were ever built. The vehicle's low-velocity 150-mm artillery howitzer was mounted in a simple slab-sided armored casemate, open at the rear. *Aberdeen Proving Grounds Museum*

combat maneuvers, they were soon immobilized because of the lack of air cover and the destructive American aerial attacks which the tanks could not counter."

The Capture of Manila

Once his forces landed on Luzon, MacArthur's greatest desire was to see his beloved city of Manila recaptured. MacArthur was so convinced that his forces could capture it quickly that his staff had already made plans for a massive victory parade through Manila. MacArthur's strong belief that Manila was his for the taking came from his intelligence chief, who had told him that Manila was basically undefended by the Japanese. What he didn't know was that, against the wishes of the Army commander in charge of all Japanese military forces on Luzon, a Japanese Rear Admiral inside Manila had decided to defend Manila on his own initiative. Under his command were roughly 20,000 men. While the majority were Marines and naval personnel, there were also a number of Japanese Army troops plus a 5,000-man force of armed Filipino collaborators.

The Japanese Rear Admiral in charge of Manila's defense was ordered to prevent MacArthur's forces from using Manila's harbor facilities and airfields as long as possible. Besides being armed with a large number of automatic weapons, the Japanese defenders of Manila were backed up with a fairly large amount of artillery. These included over 50 large Japanese 120-mm naval dual-purpose guns. The biggest shortcoming among the Japanese naval personnel in Manila was the lack of any unit training in ground combat operations. Many Japanese sailors had never had any individual infantry training.

City Fighting

Cities are normally very important targets since they are the centers of politics, transportation, communication, industry, and culture. For that reason, cities have often been locations of important battles. Some of the best-

The U.S. Sixth Army counterpart to the Japanese Type 38 Ho-Ro 150-mm self-propelled howitzer was the M7 Howitzer Motor Carriage. This vehicle mounted a 105-mm howitzer on an open-topped chassis. The M7 saw widespread use with MacArthur's ground forces on both Leyte and Luzon. The M7 pictured here is advancing past American infantry on a Luzon road. Based on the chassis of the M3 and M4 medium tanks, almost 3,500 M7s were built during World War II. Besides the 105-mm howitzer, the M7 was also fitted with a .50-caliber machine gun, which is clearly seen in this photo. *Real War Photos*

known campaigns of World War II centered around the capture of cities such as Moscow, Stalingrad, Leningrad, Warsaw, Aachen, and Berlin, to name a few.

The problem for the attacker trying to capture a city is that cities tend to offer such excellent defensive positions. City buildings provide cover and concealment, limit fields of observation and fire, and block movement, especially by mechanized troops. City streets can easily canalize an attacking force and provide little room for maneuver. Thus, obstacles on streets in cities are usually more effective than those on roads in open terrain, because they are more difficult to bypass.

Another factor in city operations is the presence of civilians, often in very large numbers. Concern for the safety of noncombatants may restrict the use of firepower and limits the maneuver options available to the attacker. Furthermore, the need to support or evacuate civilians may place an added burden on the attacker's supplies.

Military units assaulting a city often become isolated, making city combat a series of vicious small-unit battles. A skilled, well-trained defender always has tactical advantages over the attacker in city fighting because he normally occupies strong, prepared defensive positions. In contrast, the attacker must expose himself in order to advance.

Despite the restrictions that city fighting can place on an attacker's artillery weapons, artillery can still play an important role in capturing a city. Artillery can destroy fortified buildings, create passages through barricades and obstacles, accompany and support infantry and tanks in the attack, and prevent counterattacks. Due to the density of cities, artillery will often be used in the direct-fire support role.

Combined arms teams composed of tanks and infantry can also be very effective in city fighting, if used properly. The armored, protected firepower of a tank can quickly neutralize enemy defensive positions with a minimal loss of life to the accompanying infantry. However, because most tank main guns cannot be depressed sufficiently to fire into basements or elevated far enough to fire into the upper floors of buildings at very close range, there are limits to their usefulness. Tanks can also

An American M4 Sherman tank is advancing on a Japanese defensive position on Luzon. Despite the large number of American and Japanese tanks on Luzon, there were very few large-scale tank battles between the two sides. The Japanese commander on Luzon did not believe that his tanks would do well in a head-on battle with superior American tanks. Instead, he divided his tanks into a number of separate units tasked with the job of delaying MacArthur's Sixth Army on its drive to Manila. *Real War Photos*

be very vulnerable in city fighting. Streets and alleys constitute ready made fire lanes for defenders. Vehicle traffic is restricted, canalized, and vulnerable to ambush and close-range fire.

When an attacker's armored vehicles are required to travel down narrow streets or streets clogged with debris, infantry are supposed to move ahead of the tanks clearing the enemy out of buildings on each side of the street. For movement down wider streets infantry units normally have the support of at least two attached tanks with one tank on each side of a street. Other tanks normally follow the infantry and fire at targets in the upper stories of nearby buildings.

By the first week of February 1945, MacArthur had three divisions poised in the suburbs of Manila. So easy had this phase of the operation progressed that MacArthur had

In the Cabarvan Hills of Luzon these M4 Sherman tanks, supported by infantry, are advancing on Japanese defensive positions. Between mid-January and early February 1945, American infantry units supported by tanks, tank destroyers, and artillery managed to destroy over 200 tanks of the Japanese 2nd Armored Division in a series of fierce battles. The remaining tanks of the 2nd Armored Division were lost in further piecemeal holding actions. With all of its tanks destroyed, the 2nd Armored Division survivors were converted into an under-strength infantry division. *Patton Museum*

his staff prematurely release an official announcement on February 6th that Manila was now in American hands. This news was picked up by the American press and much to MacArthur's dismay and embarrassment, published before it could be rescinded.

Manila the City

Manila, including its suburbs, covered an area of almost 110 square miles and contained over 1,100,000 people. While much of the housing in Manila's suburbs was of rather flimsy construction, the buildings of Manila's business and government district were built of heavily-reinforced concrete and would prove to be excellent defensive strong-points for the Japanese defenders in the city.

To improve the defensive ability of Manila's concrete buildings, the Japanese took to fortifying building entrances with sandbags. They would also barricade interior corridors and stairways of every building. Firing slits for rifles and machine guns were chopped into the

flanks of every building. Tunnels were dug by the Japanese to connect the basements of various buildings or led to outside pillboxes and bunkers. The Japanese also barricaded almost every street and intersection throughout the downtown section of Manila with all types of obstacles, including: oil drums filled with dirt or cement; rails set into the pavement; hastily dug ditches; trolley cars, trucks, and cars; even heavy factory machinery ripped from its mounting were piled up in Manila's streets to slow down MacArthur's forces. All of these barricades were laced together by thousands upon thousands of mines and booby traps.

Hampered by often contradicting intelligence reports, MacArthur and his field commanders didn't really know until early February 1945 that the Japanese definitely planned on defending Manila. Even when this information was acquired, it was still unknown what part of this very large city the Japanese would defend. Only when MacArthur's forces finally ran into the principal Japanese stronghold did they realize what a tough battle was ahead of them. At this point MacArthur, who always considered Manila home, decided that in an attempt to minimize the destruction of the city and spare the civilian population, the Army Air Forces would not be allowed to bomb or strafe the city. American artillery would also be limited to firing only at observed targets such as Japanese gun emplacements. Sadly, American infantry casualities were so high during their first attempts to storm the Japanese defensive positions in downtown Manila that the restrictions on using artillery fire in the city had to be quickly lifted. For the rest of the battle of Manila,

American artillery would be used whenever needed. Between the American and Japanese weapons, plus some large fires touched off by the fighting between enemies, Manila would be left in ruins.

House-to-House Fighting

As the soldiers of MacArthur's command drove deeper into the heart of Manila in a steady war of attrition with the Japanese defenders, they developed a system by which they could take enemy strong-points with a minimum of casualties. Small units of American infantry would work their way from one building to the next, usually trying to secure

Knocking a path through the Luzon underbrush, an M4 Sherman tank is followed by infantry. Normally after the first assault wave of American tanks passed through a Japanese defensive position, it was the job of the supporting tanks to knock out any pillboxes missed by the first wave. It was also necessary for the second wave of tanks to cover the first wave of assault tanks by using their machine guns and canister rounds to keep enemy tank-hunting teams from sneaking up on the rear of the first assault waves of tanks. *Real War Photos*

the roof and top floor first, often by coming through the upper floors of an adjoining structure. Using stairways as axes of advance, lines of supply, and routes of evacuation, American soldiers would then begin working their way down through the building. Generally, squads of 10 men would break up into small assault teams, with one team holding entrances and perhaps the ground floor. When an entrance had been achieved, the other men of the squad would try to clear the building of enemy defenders. In many cases where American sol-

diers ran into blocked staircases and corridors they would go around the obstacle by blowing or chopping holes through adjoining walls or floors. The use of hand grenades, flame throwers, and demolitions usually helped speed up the process.

An example of the difficulties faced by MacArthur's soldiers in trying to capture some of the larger public buildings in Manila is detailed in the U.S. Army's official history of World War II: "The fight for the General Post Office, conducted simultaneously with that for

Typical of the types of Japanese artillery pieces pressed into the role of antitank weapons was the 75-mm Field Gun Model 38 (1905), two of which are seen in this picture being examined by American soldiers. In the foreground is a captured example of the Japanese 37-mm antitank gun M94. Due to a lack of experience in developing their own weapons, many Japanese weapons were direct or modified copies of German- or French-designed weapons. *Real War Photos*

the City Hall, was especially difficult because of the construction of the building and the nature of the interior defenses. A large five-story structure of earthquake-proof, heavily reinforced concrete, the Post Office was practically impervious to direct artillery, tank, and tank destroyer fire. The interior was so compartmented by strong partitions that even a 155-mm shell going directly through a window did relatively little damage inside. The Japanese had heavily barricaded all rooms and corridors, had protected their machine gunners and riflemen with fortifications seven feet high and ten sandbags thick, had strung barbed wire throughout, and even had hauled a 105-mm artillery piece up to the second floor. The building was practically impregnable to anything except prolonged, heavy air and artillery bombardment. . . . For three days XIV Corps and 37th Division Artillery pounded the Post Office, but each time troops of the 1st Battalion, 145th Infantry, attempted to enter, the Japanese drove them out. Finally, on the morning of 22 February, elements of the 1st

The regular Japanese heavy machine gun was a 1914 Hotchkiss type, gas-operated and air-cooled. Eight were issued to a machine-gun company. It was supposedly useful for directed fire up to 1,200 meters and for indirect barrage fire for another 1,000 meters. The total weight of the gun on its standard four-legged mount was 127 pounds. The rate of fire was 400 rounds a minute. Ammunition was normally fed from the left side in 30-round strips. Shown here are American Marines with a captured Japanese 1914 Hotchkiss heavy machine gun. *Real War Photos*

Shown firing at Japanese positions on Luzon is this battery of American 105-mm howitzers. For most of the campaigns fought in the Pacific during World War II, Japanese soldiers were continually amazed at the effectiveness and firepower of American artillery units. American artillery formations could often sustain concentrations of up to 200 rounds per minute for 15-minute intervals. This was a feat that Japanese artillery formations never achieved during the war. *MacArthur Memorial*

To defend themselves from the small Japanese grenade launchers (nicknamed knee mortars), U.S. Army units in the jungles of the Southwest Pacific set up their own mortars, as shown here, at the rear and center of each platoon at each halt, and laid down counter mortar fire on suspected Japanese positions. Once a direct hit was made on one of the Japanese knee mortars, it tended to discourage the Japanese mortar men from opening fire so often. *U.S. Army*

Battalion gained a secure foothold, entering through a second story window. The Japanese who were still alive soon retreated into the large dark basement, where the 145th Infantry's troops finished off organized resistance on the 23d."

The Assault on Intramuros

The last Japanese strong-point in Manila that had to be taken by MacArthur's forces before the city could be freed from the Japanese occupiers was the old walled city of Intramuros. Originally located on the edge of Manila Bay, Intramuros was bordered on three sides by an old moat and had been converted into a public park and golf course. In the center of Intramuros was an old Spanish stone fort built in 1590. Knowing that the Japanese had built an elaborate tunnel system under the old walled city which would allow them to move their troops around safe from American shellfire, MacArthur's field commanders decided to launch two simultaneous assaults on Intramuros from different directions. This would both help confuse the Japanese defenders as well as force them to divide their forces in response.

To help them in their assault on Intramuros, MacArthur's field commanders requested that he lift his ban on the use of air support in the capture of Manila. MacArthur would not change his mind. In a radio message to his field commanders, MacArthur stated: "The use of air [support] on a part of a city occupied by a friendly and allied population is unthinkable. The inaccuracy of this type of bombardment would result beyond question in the death of thousands of innocent civilians. It is not believed moreover that this would appreciably lower our own casualty rate although it would unquestionably hasten the conclusion of the operations. For these reasons I do not approve the use of air bombardment on the Intramuros district."

MacArthur's field commanders would not be deterred in their quest to use as much American firepower on Intramuros as possible. Since MacArthur had approved the use of artillery in the battle for Manila, the American officers in charge of the assault on Intramuros decided to employ all available corps and division artillery, from 240-mm howitzers on down. In addition, every tank and self-propelled 105-mm howitzer that could be found was brought forward to provide point-blank fire support for the planned attack. Heavy and light machine guns plus mortars of all sizes would also be brought to bear on Intramuros. Just how Filipino citizens trapped inside Intramuros by the Japanese defenders would survive the coming American artillery bombardment was never answered. It also seemed that MacArthur never asked that question of his field commanders.

To help soften up Japanese defensive positions prior to the actual infantry assault on the old walled city, American 8-inch howitzers with indirect fire began blasting a breach in the east wall of Intramuros on February 17, 1945. In conjunction with other artillery pieces, the American preparation bombardment of Intramuros lasted

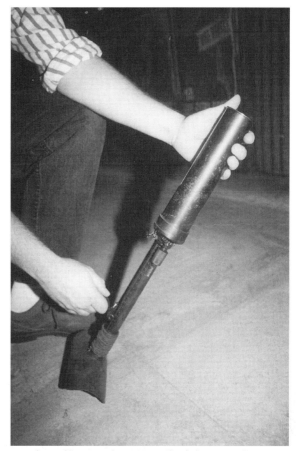

MacArthur's soldiers were always impressed with the accuracy the Japanese soldiers attained with their small grenade launchers. The Japanese grenade launcher (also called a heavy grenade thrower or knee mortar) was actually a very light and simplified 10-pound mortar. Easily carried by one man who could handle a good supply of ammunition as well, six were issued to each company. It had a short tube attached to a small adjustable shaft which rested on a broad base shoe. Because it was so light, it could be aimed and fired by one man in a pinch. Shown in its firing position is a deactivated unit on display in a private military museum. *Michael Green*

until the early morning of February 23. At 8:30 A.M. that same morning, American infantry were sent in to root out any surviving Japanese defenders.

From the postwar "Reports of General MacArthur" comes this description of the fighting for Intramuros: "The heaviest fighting took place in the sector assigned to the 37th Division. The Japanese in this area struck out viciously from every position, fighting from building to building and from room to room without surrender. It was not until 17 February that the division was able to launch its assault on the Intramuros, the 16th century walled citadel located in Western Manila near

U.S. soldiers of MacArthur's Sixth Army pass by a knocked-out Japanese armored truck. While part of MacArthur's forces were engaged in a bloody four-month struggle to drive the Japanese defenders out of the mountains of Luzon, the bulk of MacArthur's forces were sent southward down the open terrain and paved highways of the Luzon Central Plain directly toward Manila. *Real War Photos*

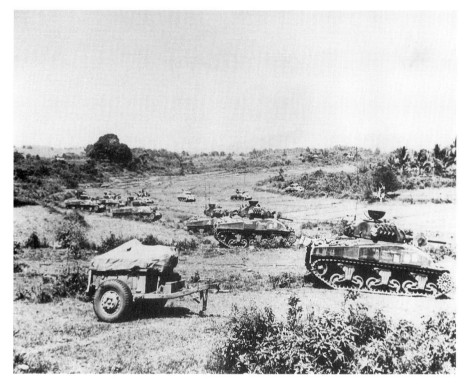

Pictured somewhere on Luzon is a company of American M4 Sherman tanks from the Army's 775th Tank Battalion. To MacArthur's surprise, the Japanese had made little effort to slow down the U.S. Army divisions bearing down on Manila. Unknown to MacArthur, the Japanese commander on Luzon had already decided that his forces stood no chance of defeating the Americans in open combat. The best of his troops had been sent to Leyte, where they had been decimated by America's gross advantage in firepower, and he had not received any reinforcements from Japan prior to MacArthur's invasion of Luzon. *Real War Photos*

the mouth of the Pasig River. Even by modern standards this ancient walled city was a formidable fortress, ringed with a stone wall 15 feet high and widening from 8 to 20 feet at the top to 20 to 40 feet at the base. Four of the main gates were covered by mutually protecting redoubts backed by a heavily fortified concrete building. . . . The attack [American] started with 105-mm and 155-mm howitzer shells blasting huge chunks out of the ancient walls. On the 19th, under cover of a heavy smoke screen, 37th Division troops began to pour through the breaches and over the rubble to meet the waiting Japanese. The enemy positions in the immediate vicinity of the walls had been effectively destroyed by the terrific power of the preliminary bombardment, and the initial incursions of the American forces met with comparatively light losses. Resistance mounted swiftly, however, as the troops advanced. To add to the difficulty, movement became greatly impeded by the streams of refugees that swarmed out of the buildings and milled around the streets. Fire had to be withheld until these scattered masses of civilians could be removed from the battle zone."

The artillery had done its work well. The walled city of Intramuros and the old Spanish

fort within it were all but demolished. There was still some scattered resistance by the surviving Japanese defenders who had to be rooted out by the American soldiers with phosphorous grenades, demolitions, bazookas, and flame throwers. By March 3, 1945, all organized resistance in the Manila area had ceased. Unfortunately, the citizens of Manila paid a very heavy price for their freedom from the Japanese. It was estimated that almost 100,000 Filipinos died before the last Japanese defensive position in Manila had been overrun. American casualties were only 1,010 killed and another 6,575 wounded. Japanese losses were estimated to be roughly 17,000 dead with the other 3,000 escaping from Manila into the surrounding mountains.

The Capture of Corregidor

As Manila was being destroyed in order to free it from the defending Japanese troops, MacArthur turned his attention to the recapture of Bataan and the island of Corregidor. Without occupying both of these spots MacArthur's naval support ships couldn't use Manila Bay. Since the Japanese commander on Luzon had already decided that trying to defend Bataan made no tactical sense,

MacArthur's forces met little enemy resistance in overrunning Bataan. The recapture of the island of Corregidor proved to be a much tougher job for MacArthur's troops.

As a prelude to the assault on Corregidor, the island and its Japanese defenders had been pounded steadily from the sea and air since the last week in January 1945.

Due to faulty intelligence work, MacArthur was led to believe that there were only 900 Japanese soldiers based on Corregidor. In fact, there were almost 5,000 Japanese soldiers prepared to die defending the island. The assault on Corregidor began when 1,000 soldiers from the 503rd Airborne Regiment parachuted onto the western half of the island on the morning of February 16, 1945. Taken by surprise, the Japanese defenders failed to inflict any casualties on the American paratroopers.

An hour or so after the paratroopers were dropped on Corregidor, another force of 1,000 American soldiers from the 34th Regimental Combat Team were landed by water on the southwest part of the island. This assault also caught the Japanese defenders by surprise. The Japanese eventually reacted to the seaborne assault and made later landings very costly for MacArthur's men.

On the afternoon of the 16th, another 1,000 troops were air-dropped on Corregidor. This time the element of surprise was gone. The Japanese defenders on Corregidor were ready and waiting. Japanese fire caused heavy losses among the second wave of parachutists of the 503rd Airborne. A third airborne assault planned for Corregidor on the same day was canceled due to the very high casualty rate. Instead, these troops were landed on the island by boat on the 17th.

The decision by MacArthur to employ one

Taking cover behind a fence on Luzon, American soldiers wait for the order to advance. General Krueger's plan for retaking Manila involved an assault on the capital from two directions. The 1st Cavalry Division and the 37th Infantry Division launched the main attack from the north of Manila, while a smaller, but nonetheless strong effort, was carried out from south of the city by a combined airborne and infantry force. *Real War Photos*

of the most difficult modern military maneuvers—a coordinated parachute and amphibious attack to take Corregidor—had a lot to do with what happened to the Japanese seaborne assault of Corregidor back in May 1941, during which the Japanese landing force took heavy losses in both men and boats. In order not to repeat the same scenario with the U.S. forces as the attackers, MacArthur believed a combination paratrooper assault and amphibious landing would catch the Japanese defenders of Corregidor by surprise. It was hoped that this would result in a nearly bloodless seizure of the island.

From a report written by MacArthur's staff comes this description of the fighting on Corregidor: "The 503rd Parachute Infantry and the battalion of the 34th RCT quickly joined forces to eliminate the main system of

On February 7, 1945, MacArthur's envelopment of Manila began. By February 11, 1945, the Japanese defenders of Manila were completely surrounded. MacArthur's ground forces, assigned the mission of clearing Manila, entered the outskirts of the city on February 12, 1945. Pictured on the outskirts of Manila is an M4 Sherman tank supporting American infantry. *MacArthur Memorial*

Ignoring a dead Japanese soldier lying in the middle of the street, these U.S. soldiers and their supporting tanks advance farther into Manila. Although the Japanese defenses inside Manila were generally improvised and adapted to meet a rapidly shifting tactical situation, the tenacity and bitterness of the resistance encountered by MacArthur's troops made their seizure of central Manila an exhaustive and prolonged effort. *MacArthur Memorial*

cave and tunnel defenses running through the Malinta Hill district. The Japanese fought to the bitter end, defending each position with devastating fire. Rather than be dislodged by the irresistible onslaught of tanks, bazookas and flame throwers, they blew up many of their tunnels in suicidal desperation."

From the official U.S. Army history of World War II comes this description of the last day of serious fighting: "Shortly after 1100 on 26 February the Japanese on Corregidor executed their final, suicidal tour de force, blowing an underground arsenal at Monkey Point amid scenes of carnage on both sides. As the dust from the terrific explosions settled, a hollow appeared where a small knoll had previously stood. Debris has flown as far as Topside where one man, almost a mile from the explosion, was injured by flying rock. Other debris hit a destroyer 2,000 yards offshore. A medium tank was hurled 50 yards through the air, most of its crew killed. Bits and pieces of American and Japanese troops splattered the ground; rock slides buried alive other men of both forces. Over 200 Japanese were killed outright, while Rock Force lost some 50 men

A wartime picture shows part of the city of Manila on fire. The American assault on central Manila quickly bogged down as the Japanese defenders fought house-to-house and street-to-street. The smoke coming from fires set by Japanese soldiers and American firepower was so thick in some parts of Manila that it was impossible to continue the battle in some places. *MacArthur Memorial*

killed and 150 wounded. Medics took an hour and a half to clear the casualties from the area, and at the end of that time one medical officer, an eyewitness to the horrors, could only report: As soon as I got all the casualties off, I sat down on a rock and burst out crying. I couldn't stop myself and didn't even want to. I had seen more than a man could stand and still stay normal. . . . When I had the cases to care for, that kept me going; but after that it was too much."

On February 27, Corregidor was declared secure. MacArthur's forces counted 4,500 dead Japanese soldiers on the island. Only 20 Japanese soldiers were captured. The rest of the Japanese defenders of Corregidor were either buried in the tunnels under the island or had managed to escape the island during the fighting.

For MacArthur, the Japanese surrender of Corregidor was more than just a small tactical victory. After three years of hard campaigning,

With his helmeted head just barely peering out of the commander's hatch of his M4 Sherman tank, this tank commander directs his medium tank past a destroyed Manila streetcar. U.S. Army units advancing on Manila from the southern side of the city began their assault with a naval landing by elements of the 11th Airborne Division. This move by MacArthur's ground forces largely sealed off the possibility of any Japanese troops south of Manila joining those to the north. It provided an added bonus to MacArthur, since it also outflanked Japanese defense lines in southern Luzon. *MacArthur Memorial*

Using a thick concrete wall for protection, the U.S. soldiers shown here in downtown Manila use the heavy firepower provided by their BARs to keep the heads of the Japanese defenders down while their comrades attempt to approach the enemy positions. It wasn't until February 17th that the remaining Japanese defenders were forced back into the oldest section of Manila, known as the Walled City of Intramuros. *MacArthur Memorial*

Complicating the planned U.S. assault on Intramuros was the fact that untold thousands of Philippine civilians were hiding within that part of the city. To minimize civilian casualties, MacArthur ordered that there be no aerial bombardment of that section of the city. American soldiers were forced to take Intramuros in a time-consuming infantry assault supported only by artillery. Pictured in downtown Luzon are Philippine civilians trying to flee with their possessions while the city burns around them. *MacArthur Memorial*

it was the fulfillment of a personal crusade. On March 2, 1945, MacArthur and many members of his prewar staff attended a ceremony on Corregidor for the raising of the American flag over the small, battle-scarred island.

The capture of Corregidor did not completely secure Manila Bay. MacArthur's forces would still have to clear the southern shore of Manila Bay as well as the many small islands between Corregidor and the Luzon mainland.

Mopping Up Luzon

Despite the capture of the Philippine capital city of Manila, as well as the Bataan Peninsula and the island of Corregidor, the fighting for the island of Luzon would continue. The Japanese commander on Luzon had gathered elements of his remaining forces in the mountains of southern Luzon. These enemy forces

The walled city of Intramuros, built during the Spanish colonial era, had walls 16 feet high, 40 feet thick at the base, tapering to 20 feet at the top. U.S. artillery was quickly moved into position around Intramuros, and began a week-long softening-up bombardment of Japanese defensive positions. Shown burning out of control is one of Manila's large concrete government buildings. *MacArthur Memorial*

would remain a threat to the recently liberated city of Manila because they could destroy the dams that supplied water to the city. They were also in a position to counterattack MacArthur's men around Manila.

On March 5, 1945, MacArthur ordered his 1st Cavalry and 6th Infantry Divisions to capture the areas around the dams. On March 8, after a heavy two-day aerial bombardment of the objective, MacArthur launched his forces. Japanese resistance was fierce and U.S. progress was slow. A communiqué issued by MacArthur's staff describes the formidable cave defenses built by the Japanese in this section of Luzon: " The enemy line of defense consists almost entirely of caves in the hillsides closely spaced for interlocking fire. A cave normally consists of a ten foot shaft large enough for a man to climb up or down a rope ladder. At the foot of the shaft a small tunnel leads to a compartment some twenty by thirty feet. Four or five lateral tunnels lead from the compartment. Just before a lateral reaches the surface slope of the hill it makes a sharp bend to prevent shelling from entering the tunnel. Against frontal assault methods the fire power developed from these miniature forts is deadly. One method of attack consists in preliminary saturating bombardments by the air, artillery and all infantry weapons calculated to confine the enemy within the tunnels. When this has been accomplished a small demolition group from the infantry moves in with white phosphorous grenades, flame throwers and demolitions. Several hundred pounds of explosive are placed inside the entrance to a lateral and blown to close the opening. In this manner the four or five laterals are sealed off and the

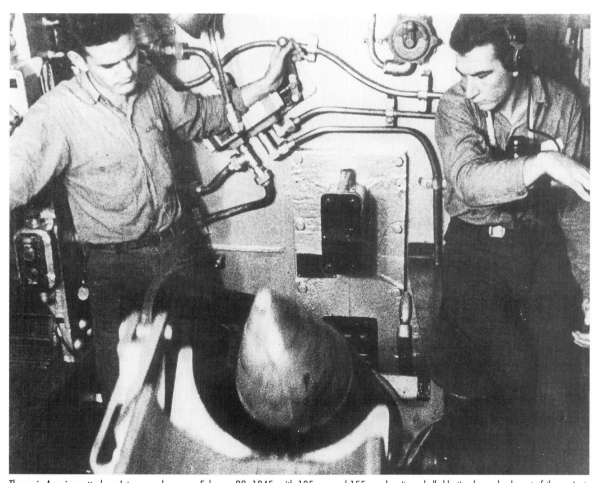

The main American attack on Intramuros began on February 23, 1945, with 105-mm and 155-mm howitzer shells blasting huge chunks out of the ancient walls. In conjunction with the artillery fire, U.S. Navy ships supporting MacArthur's invasion force opened up with a massive bombardment of their own. Pictured inside the turret of an American battleship is a large shell being hoisted into position prior to being slammed into the breech end of one of the ship's massive 16-inch guns. *Real War Photos*

vertical shaft then blown from the top. Each cave with its laterals can hold about twenty-five men. When trapped in this way the enemy is suffocated to death and destroyed without taking any compensating toll from the troops. As an example, a Brigade of the 1st Cavalry Division in forty-eight hours in the attack now developed took 137 caves and blew 446 of the outlets to these caves with practi-cally no loss themselves, while the enemy's loss is estimated at several thousand men. Similar methods have been used throughout the New Guinea and the Philippine campaigns. Progress of the attack is slowed by these methods but an enormous saving in life and materiel is affected."

It would take MacArthur's forces until mid-June 1945 to clear most of the Japanese defenders

Employed in the artillery bombardment of the old Walled City of Intramuros in Manila was the M1 155-mm medium-range artillery piece such as the one pictured here. Best known by its nickname as the "Long Tom," this 155-mm gun was based on a French-designed World War I—era cannon. Modernized in between the wars, the M1 (Long Tom) cannon was fitted on a split-rail carriage carried by eight large tires, which allowed the weapon to be towed by high-speed trucks. In action, the Long Tom had a range of almost 26,000 yards. The gun's rate of fire could be as high as one round per minute. *U.S. Army*

out of the mountains of southern Luzon. While some of his forces were busy with that task, an even bigger battle was raging in the northern mountains of Luzon. It was here that the Japanese had committed the major portion of their ground forces on the island. MacArthur had directed a number of his divisions to capture the northern mountains of Luzon beginning in mid-February 1945. This campaign would last until the end of June 1945.

Cleaning Up the Philippines

As the battle for Luzon had raged, MacArthur had also sent elements of his command to capture some of the strategically situated islands of the southern Philippines as well as the island of Borneo in the former Dutch East Indies. On April 21, 1945, MacArthur had issued a communiqué describing the signifi-

The largest artillery piece employed by the U.S. Army in its assault on Intramuros in Manila was the 240-mm Howitzer M1. Developed before World War II, the 240-mm Howitzer M1 was so large and heavy that it had to be moved on two specially designed transport trailers. The barrel of the 240-mm howitzer and its recoil system were carried on one trailer, while another trailer carried the massive gun mount. When the weapon arrived at its emplacement site, it took a large crane to put the two parts of the weapon together. Pictured here in Europe is the barrel of the 240-mm howitzer being lifted by crane into its gun mount. *U.S. Army*

Corregidor had been pounded from both the air and sea since the beginning of January 1945. On February 16, 1945, MacArthur launched a coordinated airborne and seaborn invasion force against what was left of the once-powerful island fortress of Corregidor. A battalion of Parachute Infantry made the first assault, dropping on the western portion of the island. Pictured here are two American paratroopers on Corregidor looking for Japanese holdouts. *MacArthur Memorial*

After a 90-minute bombardment of Intramuros, and under cover of a heavy smoke screen, MacArthur's troops began to enter the walled city. It took a solid week of fighting before most of Intramuros fell into American hands. However, it wasn't until March 4, 1945, that the last Japanese strong-point was overrun. Pictured inside the city of Manila is the crew of a 37-mm antitank gun blasting away at a Japanese strong-point. *MacArthur Memorial*

cance of these operations, including this excerpt: "In addition to the main islands of Leyte, Samara, Mindoro, Pane, Paladin, Negros, Bohol and Masbate, Japanese garrisons on a score of lesser islands . . . have been eliminated. This sweep clears the center of the Philippines and leaves the only remaining enemy organized resistance in Mindanao on the south and upper Luzon on the north."

The island of Mindanao was invaded by MacArthur's forces on April 17, 1945. Organized Japanese resistance on the island lasted until June 30, 1945. However, it took until mid-August 1945 to round up the last Japanese stragglers hiding in the island's mountains.

In a special communiqué to the press on July 5, 1945, MacArthur announced: "The entire Philippine Islands are now liberated and the Philippine Campaign can be regarded as virtually closed. Some minor isolated action of a guerrilla nature in the practically uninhabited mountain ranges may occasionally persist but this great land mass of 115,600 square miles with a population of 17,000,000 is now freed of the invader. The enemy during the operations employed twenty-three divisions, all of which were practically annihilated. Our forces comprised seventeen divisions. This was one of the rare instances when in a long campaign a ground force superior in numbers was entirely destroyed by a numerically inferior

A relatively new weapon in the U.S. Army's inventory that was used during the assault on Corregidor was the 57-mm recoilless rifle. Because this type of weapon required no recoil mechanism or any type of compensating mechanisms, it was very light (under 50 pounds).With this light weight and heavy punch, it was the perfect weapon for infantry and airborne units. Pictured on Corregidor is an American paratrooper aiming his recoilless rifle at a Japanese position. *MacArthur Memorial*

The airborne assault on Corregidor was quickly followed by a suborn landing of an Army battalion near MacArthur's old 1942 headquarters on Manila Hill. Looking over the shoulder of an American soldier on Corregidor, this picture shows one of the 12-inch coast artillery guns placed on Corregidor by the American military in the early 1900s. By the time MacArthur's troops returned to Corregidor in February 1945, the Japanese were using these derelict gun positions only as shelters from the American preinvasion bombardment. *MacArthur Memorial*

On the afternoon of February 16th, a second battalion of airborne infantry was dropped on Corregidor. Japanese fire, in conjunction with some very rough terrain in the drop zone, caused heavy casualties among the Army parachutists landed in the second assault. A proposed third airborne assault on Corregidor was scrapped. The third wave of Army parachutists was landed on Corregidor by boat the next day. Shown in this aerial shot is Corregidor covered with the white parachutes of the 503rd Airborne Regiment. The bombed-out buildings on the right side of the picture are the prewar concrete barracks of the American soldiers once stationed on the island. *MacArthur Memorial*

opponent. The Japanese ground forces comprised the following divisions or equivalents: 1st, 8th, 10th, 16th, 19th, 23rd, 26th, 30th, 100th, 102d, 103d, 105th, 2d Armored, 2d Airborne Brigade (reinforced to divisional strength), the 54th, 35th, 58th, 61st and 68th Independent Mixed Brigades (reinforced to divisional strength), three divisional units known as the Kobayashi, Suzuki and Shimbu commands, organized from twenty-eight independent battalions, three naval divisions comprising a Provisional Naval Command of corps strength, under Admirals Iwabuchi and Shiroya, and a large number of base and service elements. The total strength approximated 450,000 men.

"Naval and air forces shared equally with the ground troops in accomplishing the success of the campaign. Naval battles reduced the Japanese Navy to practical impotence and the air losses running into many thousands have seriously crippled his air potential. Working in complete unison the three services inflicted the greatest disaster ever sustained by Japanese arms."

"The objects of the campaign were as follows:

"1. To penetrate and pierce the enemy's center so as to divide him into north and south, his homeland to the north, his captured Pacific possessions to the south. Each half could then be enveloped and attacked in turn.

"2. The acquisition of a great land, sea and air base for future operations both to the north and to the south comparable to the British Islands in its use as a base for allied operations from the west against Germany.

"3. The establishment of a great strangulating air and sea blockade between Japan and the conquered possessions in the Pacific to the south so as to prevent raw materials from being sent to the north and supply or reinforcement to the south.

"4. The liberation of the Philippines with the consequent collapse of the enemy's imperial concept of a Greater East Asia Co-Prosperity Sphere and the reintroduction of democracy in the Far East.

"5. The liberation of our captured officers and men and of internees held in the Philippines.

It took MacArthur's troops 12 bloody days of fighting to retake Corregidor from its 5,000 Japanese defenders, most of whom died in the fighting rather than surrender. American casualties were 210 dead and about 1,000 wounded. With his talent for showmanship MacArthur decided to return to Corregidor on March 2, 1945, the same way he left in March 1942, by PT Boat. This picture shows MacArthur on his arrival at Corregidor's main dock. In the background is MacArthur's staff awaiting their turn to step onto the island they left with MacArthur three years before. *MacArthur Memorial*

After his return to Corregidor on March 2, 1945, MacArthur spent some of his time touring the ruins of his old headquarters. After his quick tour of the island, MacArthur and his staff proceeded to the former main parade field of Corregidor. In a dramatic ceremony performed around Corregidor's old flag pole, the commander of the 503rd Airborne Regiment presented the captured island to MacArthur. After awarding the commander of the Airborne unit a Distinguished Service Cross, MacArthur ordered the U.S. flag raised over Corregidor once again. This picture shows the ceremony just as the flag was being raised. *MacArthur Memorial*

On March 10, 1945, MacArthur sent elements of his 41st Infantry Division to land on Mindanao, the second-largest island in the Philippines. Mindanao had originally been the first target for MacArthur's invasion of the Philippines. While initial Japanese resistance to the American landing was very light, as soon as MacArthur's troops moved into the island's interior, Japanese resistance got increasingly fierce. Pictured here are American soldiers in their landing craft waiting for the naval bombardment to end before making their run onto enemy shores. *U.S. Navy*

"6. A crippling blow to the Japanese Army, Navy, and Air Force.

"All of these purposes were accomplished."

While MacArthur was very pleased with his return to the Philippines as the conquering hero, the typical American soldier was not as cheerful about the campaign to liberate the Philippines. A campaign that MacArthur had promised Washington would only take six weeks with light losses, and would cause the Japanese to end the war, instead took six months and cost almost 50,000 American soldiers killed or wounded. Japanese causalities were estimated to be almost 200,000 killed or wounded. Total Filipino civilian dead and wounded are unknown.

Shown at the moment of firing is an American 57-mm antitank gun in the Philippines. Copied from a British-designed weapon, this 2,810-pound gun could hurl a 6-pound shell to a maximum range of 10,260 yards. With the ability to fire only solid shot, the 57-mm gun was mainly used to destroy Japanese bunkers and pillboxes. Despite the capture of Manila and Corregidor, and with most of the remaining Japanese cut off from resupply and reinforcements, MacArthur insisted that his ground forces root out every Japanese soldier in the Philippines rather then let them starve to death or die of disease. *Real War Photos*

Even as his troops were locked in fierce combat on Luzon, MacArthur asked the Joint Chiefs if he could mount invasions of both the Japanese-occupied islands of Borneo and Java. The Joint Chiefs saw no need to invade the heavily defended island Java, but they reluctantly gave MacArthur permission to invade Borneo. With all of his U.S. Army divisions already committed to other actions, MacArthur assigned the task of invading and occupying Borneo to an all-Australian force commanded by Australian General Sir Thomas Blamey. Shown in this aerial shot is the Japanese-held island of Borneo being attacked by American aircraft. *U.S. Navy*

There were three Australian landings on Borneo, the first one on May 1, 1945, followed by a second one on June 10. The last Australian landing on Borneo was on July 1st. This was also the last amphibious landing in World War II. Pictured coming out the front end of a U.S. Navy LCT on a Borneo beach are Australian troops with their familiar wide-brimmed slough hats. Except for some minor mopping-up operations, Borneo would be under almost-complete Australian control by early July 1945. *U.S. Navy*

Chapter Five

THE END OF THE WAR IN THE PACIFIC

Even as MacArthur's forces were battling it out with the Japanese in the Philippines, the Joint Chiefs of Staff had already begun the planning for the invasion of Japan.

On February 9, 1945, the Joint Chiefs presented to both President Roosevelt and British Prime Minister Winston Churchill their strategic conclusions on how best to end the war in the Pacific. The proposed objectives would include:

a. Following the Okinawa operation, to seize additional positions to intensify the blockade and air bombardment of Japan in order to create a situation favorable to:

b. An assault on Kyushu for the purpose of further reducing Japanese capabilities by containing and destroying major enemy forces and further intensifying the blockade and air bombardment in order to establish a tactical condition favorable to:

c. The decisive invasion of the industrial heart of Japan through the Tokyo Plain.

In late March 1945, the Joint Chiefs, working on the assumptions that the war with Nazi Germany would soon be over and the planned invasion of the Japanese-held island of Okinawa would be completed by mid-August 1945, set a tentative schedule for the invasion of Japan. The cover name for the planned invasion was "Downfall" and consisted of two main operations: "Olympic," the preliminary assault on the southern Japanese island of Kyushu, which was slated for December 1, 1945, and "Coronet," the subsequent landing on the Japanese island of Honshu, which was scheduled for March 1, 1946.

While MacArthur's forces engaged in the recapture of the Philippines, Nimitz's forces were conducting their own campaigns. On February 19, 1945, two Marine Corps divisions were landing on the island of Iwo Jima under cover of Nimitz's Third Fleet. The island was an important objective for the advance on the Japanese home islands since it was only two hours' flight time from Japan. Pictured on the beach at Iwo Jima are the destroyed remains of two Marine Corps LVT(A)2s and a M4 Sherman tank that lost a track to a land mine. *U.S. Navy*

In early April 1945, the Joint Chiefs told MacArthur to wrap up his operations in the Philippines and begin making plans and preparations for the invasion of Japan.

MacArthur's views on the capture of Japan revolved around three possible courses of action. First, the Allies could encircle Japan and use their massive air power advantage to level the islands of Kyushu and Honshu and then land the American invasion force. A second option that MacArthur suggested was to isolate Japan completely by capturing bases to the west of it and bomb her into submission without actually landing any American soldiers on the Japanese home islands. The third idea MacArthur had was to attack the island of Kyushu directly and build enough airfields to support a large land-based air fleet which could cover a decisive assault against the principal island of Honshu.

Eventually, MacArthur decided that his third choice made the most sense. In his own words: "It would attain neutralization by establishing air power at the closest practicable distance from the final objective in the Japanese islands; would permit application of full power of our combined resources, ground, naval, and air, on the decisive objective; would deliver an attack against an area which probably will be more lightly defended this year than next; would continue the offensive methods which have proved so successful in Pacific campaigns; would place maximum pressure of our combined forces upon the enemy, which might well force his surrender earlier than anticipated; and would place us in the best favorable position for delivery of the decisive assault early in 1946. Our attack would have to be launched with a lessor degree of neutralization and with a shorter period of time for preparation."

Organized Japanese resistance on Iwo Jima ended on March 16, 1945. Almost all of Iwo Jima's 22,000 Japanese soldiers died defending the island. The Marines suffered close to 19,000 casualties with almost 7,000 men killed. Pictured guarding a captured Japanese bunker on Iwo Jima is a Marine. Sticking out of the bunker's opening is a Japanese 120-mm coast artillery gun. The captured airfield on Iwo Jima played an important part in the air offensive against Japan. It acted as an emergency stopping point for American heavy bombers as well as a base for shorter-range fighter planes to escort American bombers over Japan. *Real War Photos*

On May 25, 1945, the Joint Chiefs of Staff set the target date for the invasion of the Japanese island of Kysushu for November 1, 1945. MacArthur was given the primary responsibility for the invasion of Kysushu as well as the seizure of the rest of the Japanese home islands. Admiral Nimitz was given the responsibility for all naval operations plus amphibious landings in the Japanese home islands.

By the summer of 1945, it was obvious to most high-ranking military and civilian leaders in Japan that the end of the war was near. American air raids on Japan had become increasingly severe. Between April and June 1945, the Japanese had suffered an increasing series of setbacks, including the loss of the Philippines, Germany's surrender, and the American capture of the island of Okinawa. The U.S. Navy had progressively cleared the Pacific Ocean of almost all Japanese warships. Even in Tokyo Bay, Japanese warships could

Even before MacArthur's forces landed in the Philippines, Boeing B-29 Superfortresses had begun blasting the great cities of the Japanese home islands on an ever-increasing scale. Chief targets were aircraft plants, docks, and small manufacturing plants. The first B-29 raid on the Japanese home islands occurred on June 15, 1945. Pictured on the island of Guam are B-29 bombers being prepared for their next mission. *MacArthur Memorial*

Under cover of an intense naval bombardment, both U.S. Army and Marine Corps units landed on the Japanese island of Okinawa on April 1, 1945. Okinawa is only 360 miles from the Japanese main islands. The capture of Okinawa would provide airfields for U.S. planes to use in attacks on Japan. Okinawa was not declared secured until June 21, 1945. Japanese losses were over 100,000 men killed, while American wounded numbered about 36,000 men with almost 13,000 killed. Pictured on Okinawa is a Marine Corps bazooka team ready to fire at a Japanese position. *Real War Photos*

find no place to hide from the carrier-based aircraft of the U.S. Navy.

As MacArthur pushed ahead with his plans for the invasion of Japan, international negotiations were under way which ultimately would make MacArthur's projected invasion plans unnecessary. On July 26, 1945, President Harry Truman, while attending the Potsdam Conference, issued a final ultimatum to the Japanese government that gave Japan the choice of surrender or destruction. Set forth in powerful words of warning, the Potsdam Declaration read in part: "The prodigious land, sea and air forces of the United States, the British Empire and of China, many times reinforced by the armies and air fleets from the west, are poised to strike the final blows upon Japan. This military power is sustained

Pictured in this wonderful aerial view is the U.S. Navy battleship the *Mississippi* in the Pacific on July 3, 1945. By direction of the Joint Chiefs of Staff, MacArthur was appointed commander of all U.S. Army forces in the Pacific on April 6, 1945. Both he and Admiral Nimitz, commander of Naval Forces in the Pacific, were directed to prepare for the final operation against Japan. In June 1945, MacArthur created a new command known as the United States Army Forces in the Western Pacific to replace the old Southwest Pacific Area Command title. *Real War Photos*

and inspired by the determination of all the Allied Nations to prosecute the war against Japan until she ceases to resist. . . . The time has come for Japan to decide whether she will continue to be controlled by those self-willed militaristic advisors whose unintelligent calculations have brought the Empire of Japan to the threshold of annihilation, or whether she will follow the path of reason. . . ."

Japan rejected Truman's Potsdam Declaration of July 26, 1945. On August 6, 1945, a single B-29 dropped an atomic bomb on the Japanese port city of Hiroshima. On August 7, President Truman announced to the world: "Sixteen hours ago an American airplane dropped one bomb on Hiroshima, an important Japanese army base. That bomb had more power than 20,000 tons of TNT. . . . With this bomb we have now added a new and revolutionary increase in destruction to supplement the growing power of our armed forces. . . .

"It is an atomic bomb. It is a harnessing of the basic power of the universe . . .

"We are now prepared to obliterate more rapidly and completely every productive enterprise the Japanese have above ground in any city. We shall destroy their docks, their factories, and their communications. Let there be no mistake; we shall completely destroy Japan's power to make war.

Shown together in the Pacific in 1945 are the U.S. Navy fast battleships the *Missouri* and the *Iowa*. Both battleships were armed with nine 16-inch guns as well as 25 5-inch dual-purpose guns. Antiaircraft protection was provided by a large number of 40-mm and 20-mm guns. By July 1945 the warships of Nimitz's Third Fleet were sailing boldly into Japanese home waters with little or no Japanese resistance. *Real War Photos*

By July 1945, the Japanese realized that a full American invasion of the Japanese home islands was fast approaching. The Japanese began to prepare their remaining forces for a last-ditch defense of their homeland. To help stop a future American invasion fleet the Japanese built over 8,000 suicide attack planes. Looking down from the bridge of a U.S. Navy battleship, quad 40-mm antiaircraft guns are clearly visible. Battleships could have as many as 15 of these weapons. In the lower-left corner of the picture is a 20-mm antiaircraft gun; Navy battleships could be fitted with as many as 60 of these weapons. *Real War Photos*

The Japanese naval equivalent of a kamikaze plane was a wooden-hulled suicide boat known as the Shinyo. Shown here is a captured example of such a Japanese suicide boat. Packed with high explosives, these small high-speed vessels were designed to be rammed into American warships under cover of darkness. Over 6,000 were built before the war ended. *Real War Photos*

"It was to spare the Japanese people from utter destruction that the ultimatum of July 26 was issued at Potsdam."

On August 9, 1945, the Soviet Union entered the war against Japan, attacking Japanese forces in Manchuria; and on the same day another B-29 dropped a second atomic bomb on the Japanese city of Nagasaki. Next day, Japan opted for peace.

While the Japanese government considered its final acceptance of the Allied surrender terms, the Joint Chiefs of Staff plans for the occupation of Japan had already been completed. Arrangements for the hoped-for peaceful entry of Allied forces into Japan were based upon the actual invasion plans. The most immediate objectives of the Allied forces landings in Japan would be the disarming and demobilization of Japanese armed forces. Other tasks for Allied troops in Japan would include the occupation of major strategic areas such as seaports and airfields.

It was decided that final authority for the execution of the terms of surrender and for the occupation of Japan would rest with a Supreme Commander for the Allied Powers. The British, Soviet, and Chinese Governments concurred with President Truman's proposal that MacArthur be designated Supreme

Commander to assume the overall administration of the surrender.

On August 15, 1945, the Japanese sent to the United States its notification of final surrender. This message read in part:

"His Majesty the Emperor has issued an Imperial Rescript regarding Japan's acceptance of the provisions of the Potsdam declaration:

"His Majesty the Emperor is prepared to authorize and ensure the signature by his Government and the Imperial General Headquarters of the necessary terms for carrying out the provisions of the Potsdam declaration.

"His Majesty is also prepared to issue his commands to all his military, naval, and air authorities of Japan and all the forces under their control wherever located to cease active operations, to surrender arms, and to issue such orders as may be required by the Supreme Commander of the Allied Forces of the above-mentioned terms."

Shown here are U.S. Navy aircraft carriers cruising in the Pacific in 1945. On July 10, 1945, the fast carriers of the Third Fleet arrived within striking distance of the Japanese capitol of Tokyo. In the largest raid of U.S. Navy aircraft since the beginning of the Pacific War, over 1,000 carrier-based planes attacked military targets in the metropolitan Tokyo area with bombs and rockets. *Real War Photos*

As MacArthur planned for his invasion of Japan a new weapon, the atom bomb, ended the war much faster then anybody could guess. The first atomic bomb was dropped by a B-29 bomber on August 6, 1945, on the military base city of Hiroshima. Shown here is the well-known B-29 bomber the Enola Gay, which actually dropped the atomic bomb on Hiroshima. On August 9, 1945, a second atomic bomb was dropped on the Japanese port city of Nagasaki. *MacArthur Memorial*

President Truman promptly sent the Japanese Government a message which read in part: "Send emissaries at once to the Supreme Commander for the Allied Powers with information of the disposition of the Japanese forces and commanders, and fully empowered to make any arrangements directed by the Supreme Commander for the Allied Powers to enable him and his accompanying forces to arrive at the place designated by him to receive the formal surrender."

After a number of meetings between Japanese government envoys who had flown to Manila to meet with MacArthur and staff, it was arranged that the first American troops would be flown into a Japanese military air-field located 25 miles southwest of Tokyo on August 28, 1945. On August 29, Admiral Halsey's Third Fleet sailed into Tokyo Bay to prepare for the first seaborne landing on the Japanese mainland. By the evening of August 30, there were roughly 4,200 combat-equipped soldiers of the 11th Airborne Division on the ground in Japan. On September 1, 1945, MacArthur himself would fly into Japan.

On the morning of September 2, 1945, in ceremonies aboard the U.S. Navy Battleship Missouri, berthed in Tokyo Bay, Japan formally surrendered to MacArthur. At the end of the surrender ceremony, MacArthur gave one of his very typical pompous and blustery speeches that he is so well known for: "My fellow countrymen,

Being examined by U.S. Marines is a large Japanese coast artillery gun fitted with an armored shield. On August 15, 1945, the Japanese government informed the American government that it was ready to surrender. President Truman (who succeeded President Roosevelt, who died on April 12, 1945) announced that day the appointment of MacArthur as the Supreme Commander for the Allied Powers. *Real War Photos*

The first U.S. soldiers from MacArthur's command began landing in Japan on August 28, 1945. MacArthur himself landed at a large Japanese military airfield outside of Tokyo on August 30, 1945. Pictured on their arrival in Japan are MacArthur (center, wearing dark glasses) and Lt. General Robert Eichelberger (front line, 2nd from right) being escorted by other U.S. Army officers after landing in Japan. MacArthur's personal aircraft, a four-engined C-54 transport nicknamed "Bataan," stands in the background. *MacArthur Memorial*

today the guns are silent. A great tragedy has ended. A great victory has been won. The skies no longer rain death—the seas bear only commerce—men everywhere walk upright in the sunlight. The entire world is quietly at peace. The holy mission has been completed, and in reporting this to you, the people I speak for the thousands of silent lips, forever stilled among the jungles and the beaches and in the deep waters of the Pacific which marked the way. I speak for the unnamed brave millions homeward bound to take up the challenge of that future which they did so much to salvage from the brink of disaster.

"As I look back on the long tortuous trail from those grim days of Bataan and Corregidor, when an entire world lived in fear, when democracy was on the defensive everywhere when modern civilization trembled in the balance, I thank a merciful God that He has give us the faith, the courage, and the power from which to mold victory.

"We have known the bitterness of defeat and the exultation of triumph, and from both we have learned there can be no turning back. We must go forward to preserve in peace what we won in war.

"A new era is upon us. Even the lesson of victory itself brings with it profound concern, both for our future security and the survival of civilization. The destructiveness of the war potential, through progressive advances in scientific discovery, has in fact now reached a point which revises the traditional concept of war.

"Men since the beginning of time have sought peace. Various methods through the ages have attempted to devise an international process to prevent or settle disputes between nations. From the very start workable methods were found insofar as individual citizens were concerned, but the mechanics of an instrumentality of larger inter-national scope have never been successful. Military alliance, balances of power, League of Nations all in turn failed, leaving the only path to be by way of the crucible of war.

"The utter destructiveness of war now blots out this alternative. We have had our last chance. If we do not now devise some greater and more equitable system Armageddon will be at our door. The problem basically is theological and involves a spiritual recrudescence and improvement of human character that will synchronize with our almost matchless advance in science, art, literature, and all material and cultural developments of the past 2,000 years. It must be of the spirit if we are to save the flesh.

"We stand in Tokyo today reminiscent of our countryman, Commodore Perry. His purpose was to bring to Japan an era of enlightenment and progress by lifting the veil of isolation to the friendship, trade, and commerce of the world. But, alas, the knowledge thereby gained of Western science was forged into an instrument of oppression and human enslavement. Freedom of expression, freedom of action, even freedom of thought were denied through suppression of liberal education, through appeal to superstition, and through the application of force.

"We are committed by the Potsdam Declaration of Principles to see that the Japanese people are liberated from this condition of slavery. It is my purpose to implement this commitment just as rapidly as the armed forces are demobilized and other essential steps taken to neutralize the war potential. The energy of the Japanese race, if properly directed, will enable expansion vertically rather than horizontally. If the talents of the race are turned into constructive channels, the country can lift itself from its present deplorable state into a position of dignity.

"To the Pacific Basin has come the vista of a new emancipated world. Today, freedom is on the offensive, democracy is on the march. Today, in Asia as well as in Europe, unshackled peoples are tasting the full sweetness of liberty, the relief from fear.

"In the Philippines, America has evolved a model for this new free world of Asia. In the

On September 2, 1945, the formal surrender of Japan took place on the decks of the U.S. Navy's Third Fleet flagship, the battleship *Missouri*. Anchored in the middle of Tokyo Bay, the *Missouri* was protected by dozens of large and small vessels that formed a tight cordon around the surrender ship. Overhead, hundreds of U.S. Army and Navy planes maintained a protective vigil over the *Missouri*. MacArthur is seen shaking hands with some of the American officers gathered for the surrender ceremony. *Real War Photos*

This photo taken onboard the battleship *Missouri* shows MacArthur approaching the table where representatives of the Japanese government were forced to sign the formal surrender documents. Walking alongside MacArthur is Admiral Chester Nimitz. Also on the *Missouri* that day were a number of representatives of the various countries that participated in the Pacific War. Visible in the foreground are the hats of officers from both France and Great Britain. *Real War Photos*

Philippines, America has demonstrated that peoples of the East and peoples of the West may walk side by side in mutual respect and with mutual benefit. The history of our sovereignty there has now the full confidence of the East.

"And so, my fellow countrymen, today I report to you that your sons and daughters have served you well and faithfully with the calm, deliberate, determined fighting spirit of the American soldier and sailor based upon a tradition of historical trait, as against the fanaticism of any enemy supported only by mythological fiction, their spiritual strength and power has brought us through to victory. They are homeward bound—take care of them."

A civilian representative of the Japanese government signs the official surrender document on the deck of the U.S. Navy battleship, the *Missouri*. MacArthur stands opposite the table before a number of microphones. After the Japanese signed the formal surrender documents, they departed for Tokyo. Simultaneously, hundreds of Army planes and Navy planes roared over the *Missouri* in one last display of massed air might. The entire surrender ceremony took 20 minutes. *Real War Photos*

Five days after the formal Japanese surrender, MacArthur entered Tokyo and established his new headquarters in the center of the city. For the next several years MacArthur was virtual ruler of over 70 million people. He is pictured here leaving his Tokyo city headquarters. *MacArthur Memorial*

U.S. Navy personnel observe a derelict Japanese battleship in Tokyo Bay at the end of the war. In signing the surrender documents on board the U.S. Navy battleship, the *Missouri*, on August 2, 1945, the Japanese bound themselves to accept the provisions of the Potsdam Declaration, to surrender unconditionally their armed forces wherever located, to liberate all internees and prisoners of war, and to carry out all orders issued by MacArthur under the terms of surrender. *Real War Photos*

Appendix

SELECTED BIBLIOGRAPHY

Cannon, M. Hamlin. Leyte: The Return to the Philippines (The United States Army in World War II, The War in the Pacific). Washington, D.C.: Office of the Chief of Military History, 1954.

Hunt, Frazier. The Untold Story of Douglas MacArthur. New York: The Devian-Adair Company, 1954.

Miller, John, Jr. Cartwheel: The Reduction of Rabaul (The United States Army in World War II, The War in the Pacific). Washington, D.C.: Office of the Chief of Military History, 1959.

Morton, Louis. The Fall of the Philippines (The United States Army in World War II). Washington D.C.: Office of the Chief of Military History, 1953.

Morton, Louis. Strategy and Command: The First Two Years (The United States Army in World War II). Washington, D.C.: Office of the Chief of Military History, 1962.

Smith, Robert Ross. The Approach to the Philippines (The United States Army in World War II, The War in the Pacific). Washington, D.C.: Office of the Chief of Military History, 1953.

Index